This tracker belongs to

_____

Printed in the United States of America

First Printing, 2020

ISBN: 9781661197032

Burke & Bunny
P.O. Box 124
Ontonagon, Michigan 49953

burkeandbunny.com

How to use your goal tracker journal

Each day that you keep your new habit or goal going, grab some colored pencils or crayons and color in the date.

Each two-page spread has a month of circles and a month of squares, making it easy to track two new habits at a time. Or track as many as you want!

Month/year:

Goal/habit:

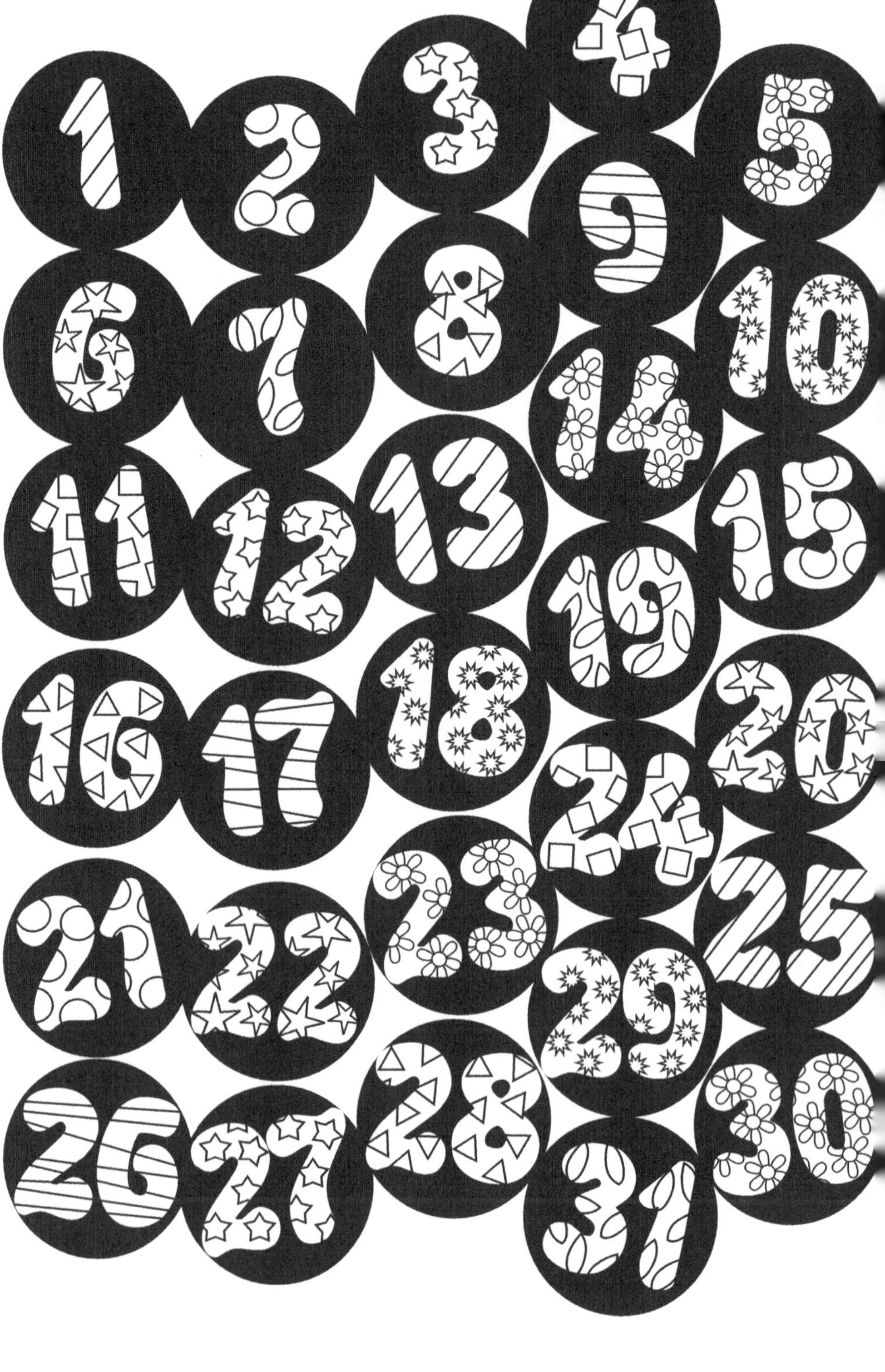

Month/year:

Goal/habit:

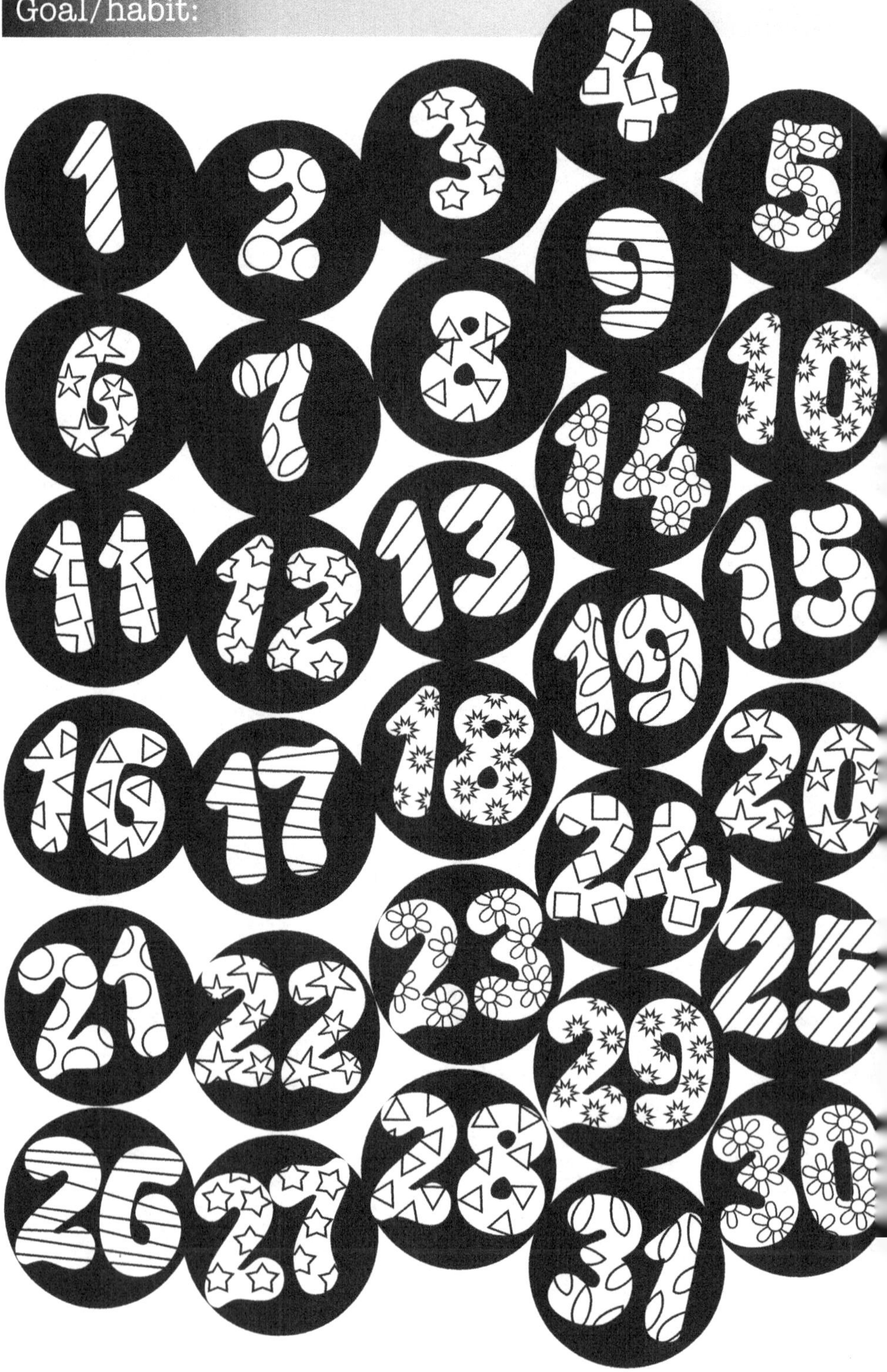

Month/year:

Goal/habit:

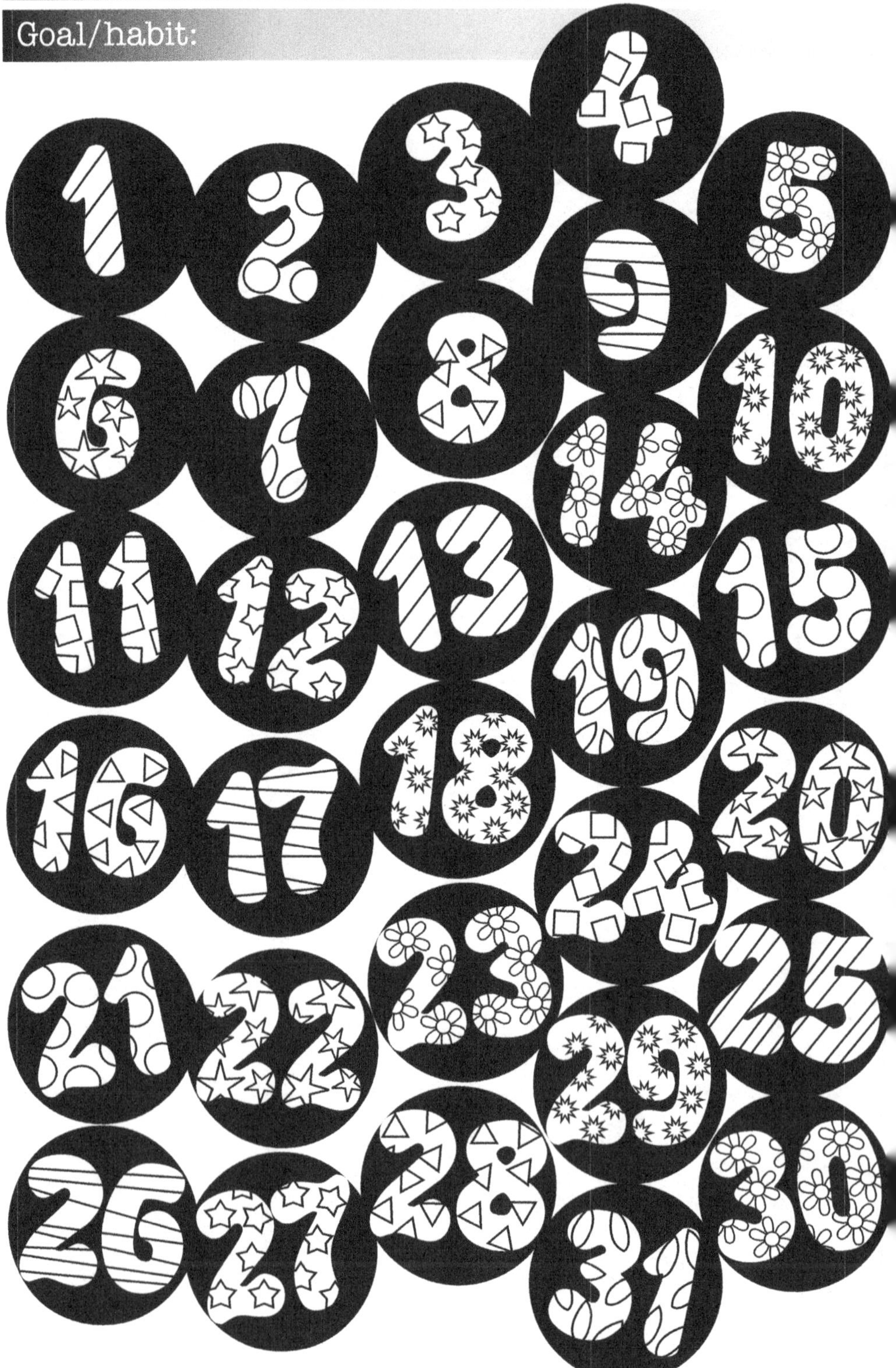

Month/year:

Goal/habit:

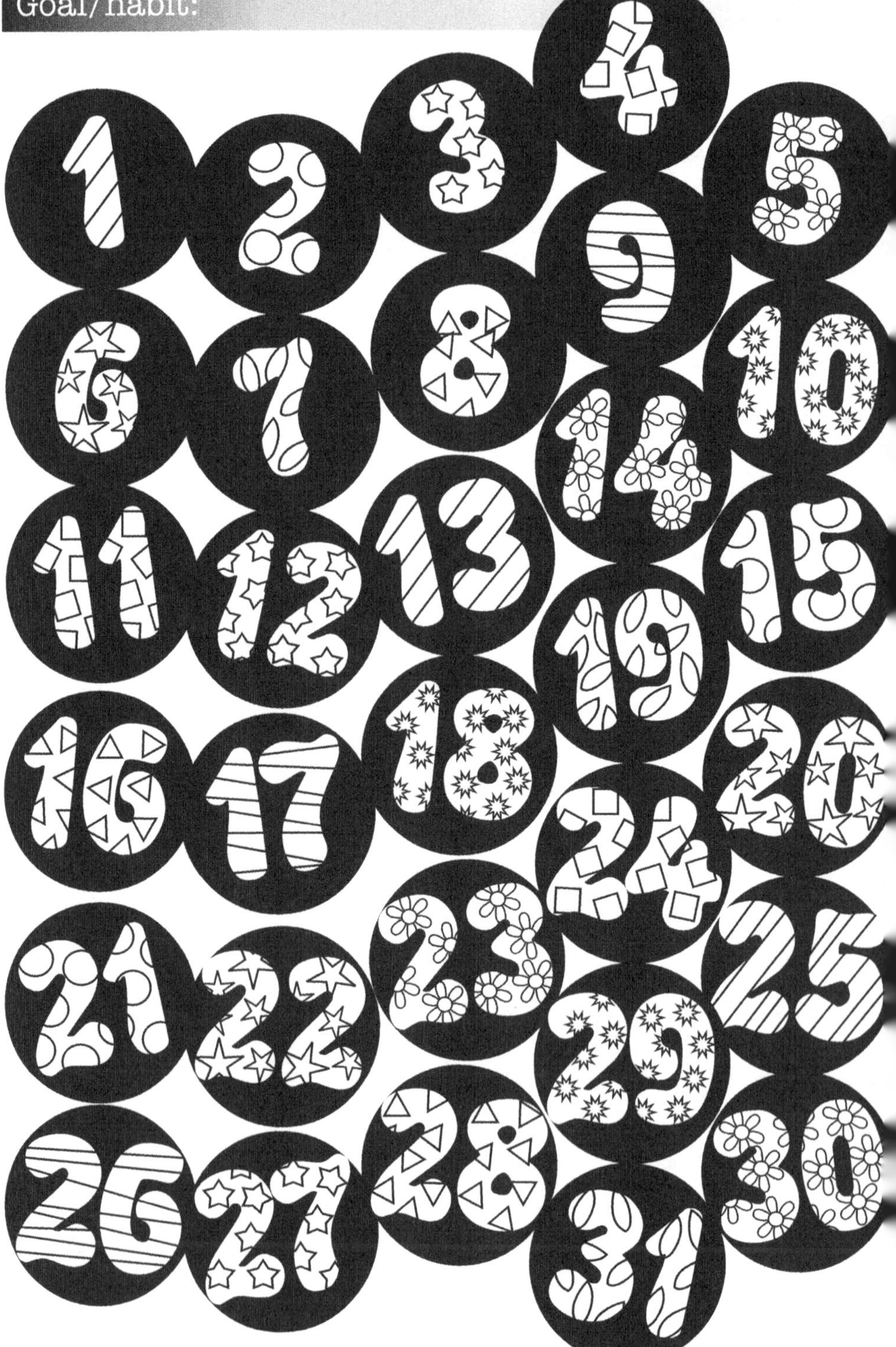

Month/year:

Goal/habit:

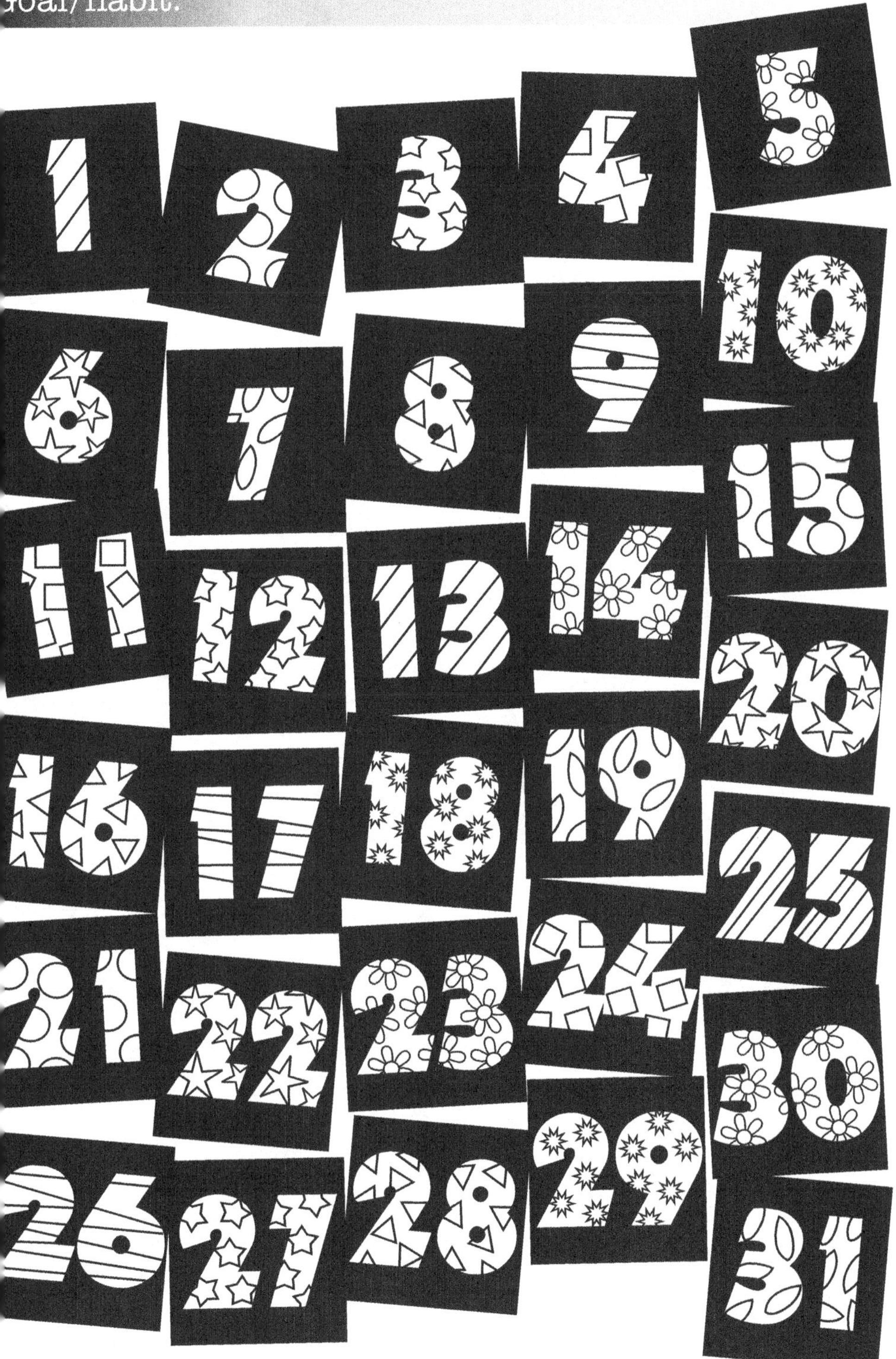

Month/year:

Goal/habit:

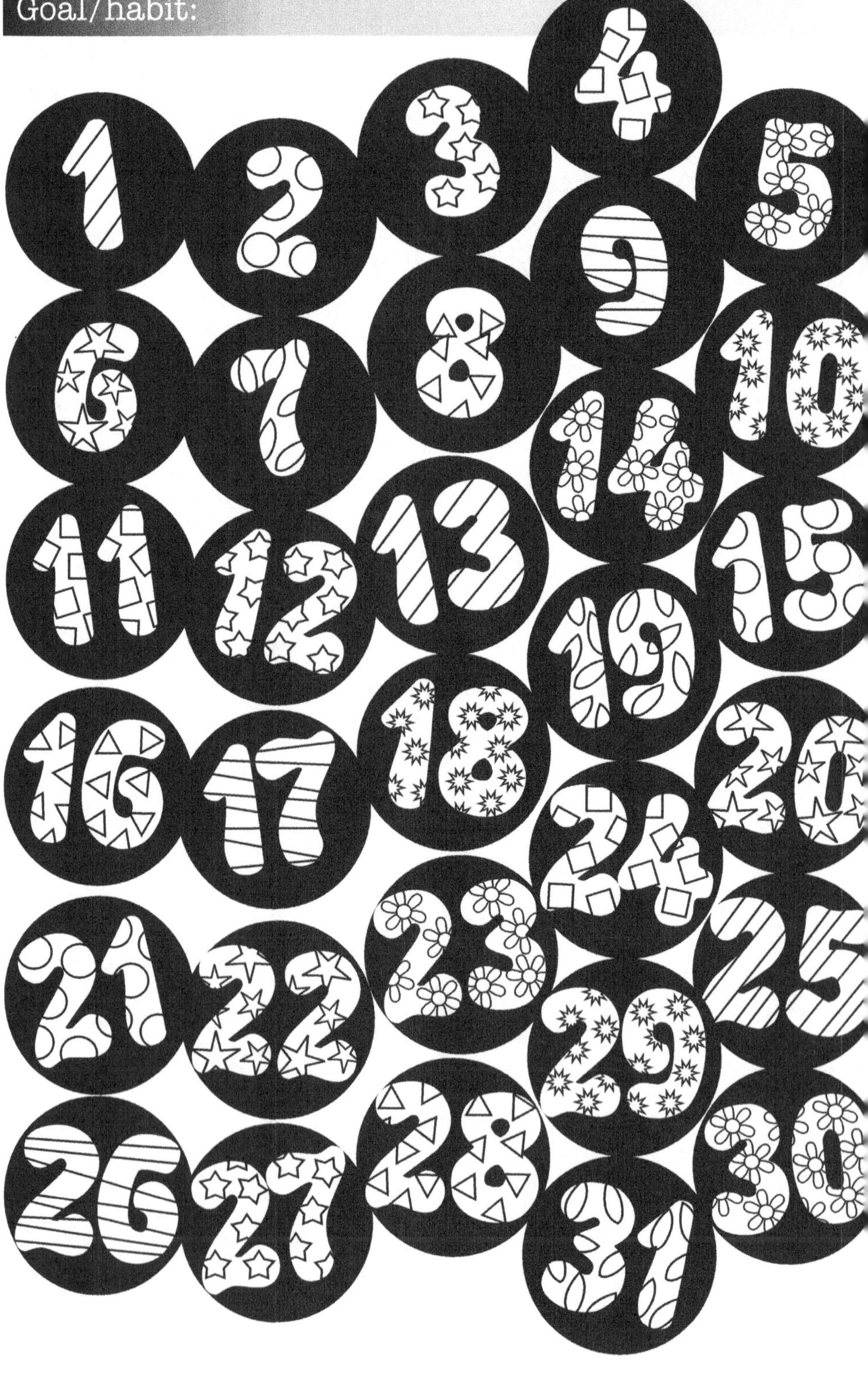

Month/year:

Goal/habit:

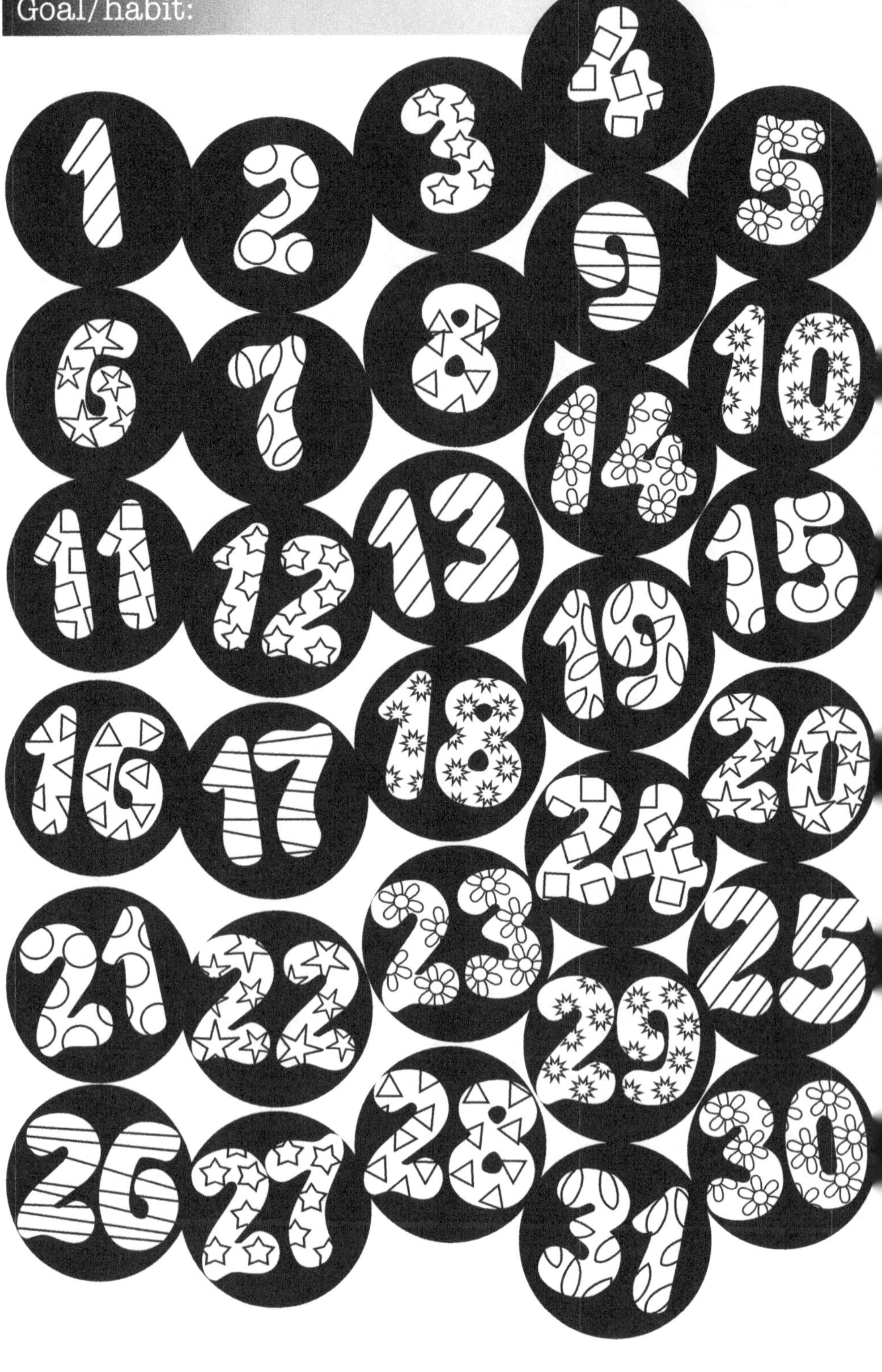

Month/year:

Goal/habit:

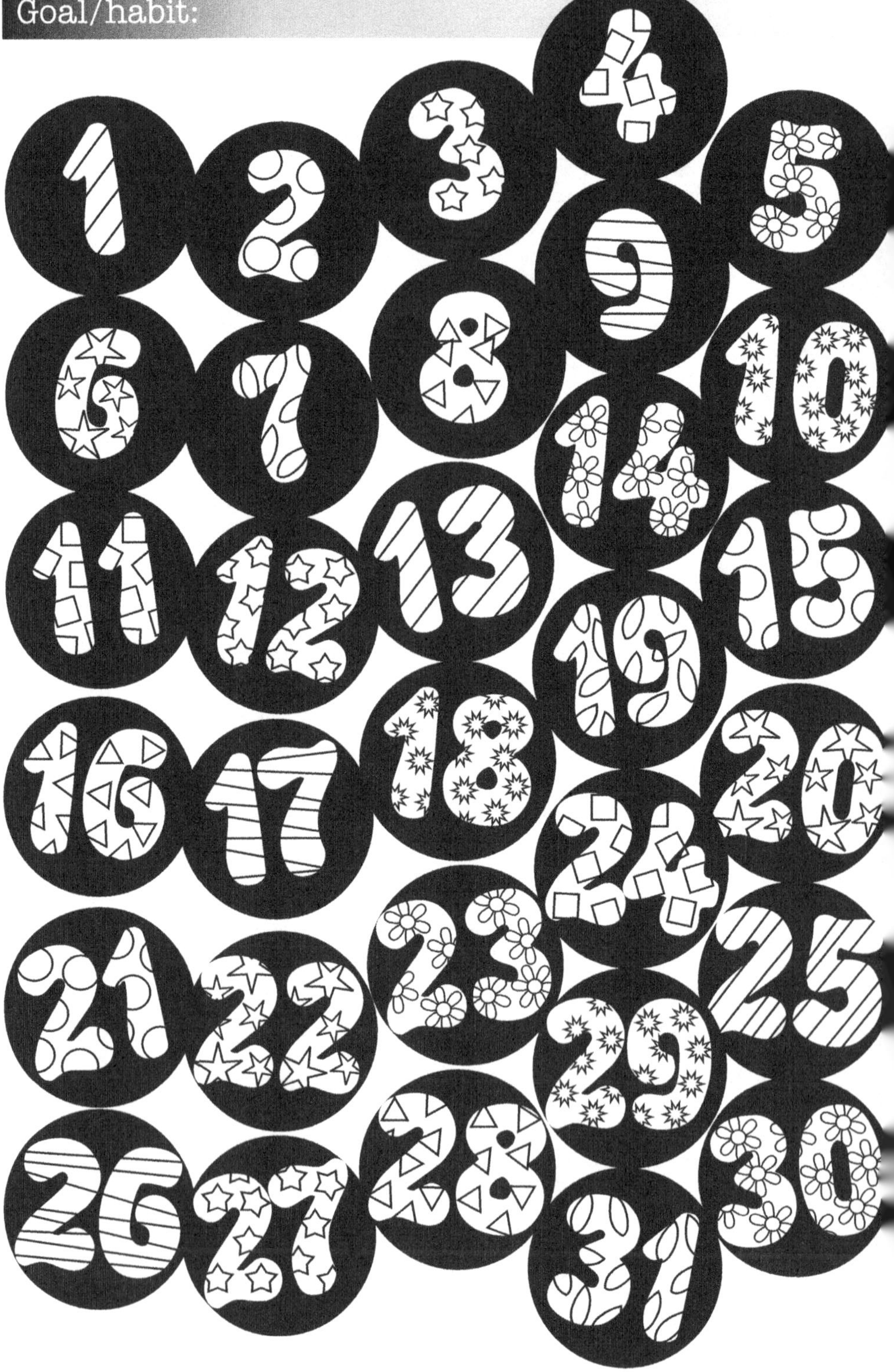

Month/year:

Goal/habit:

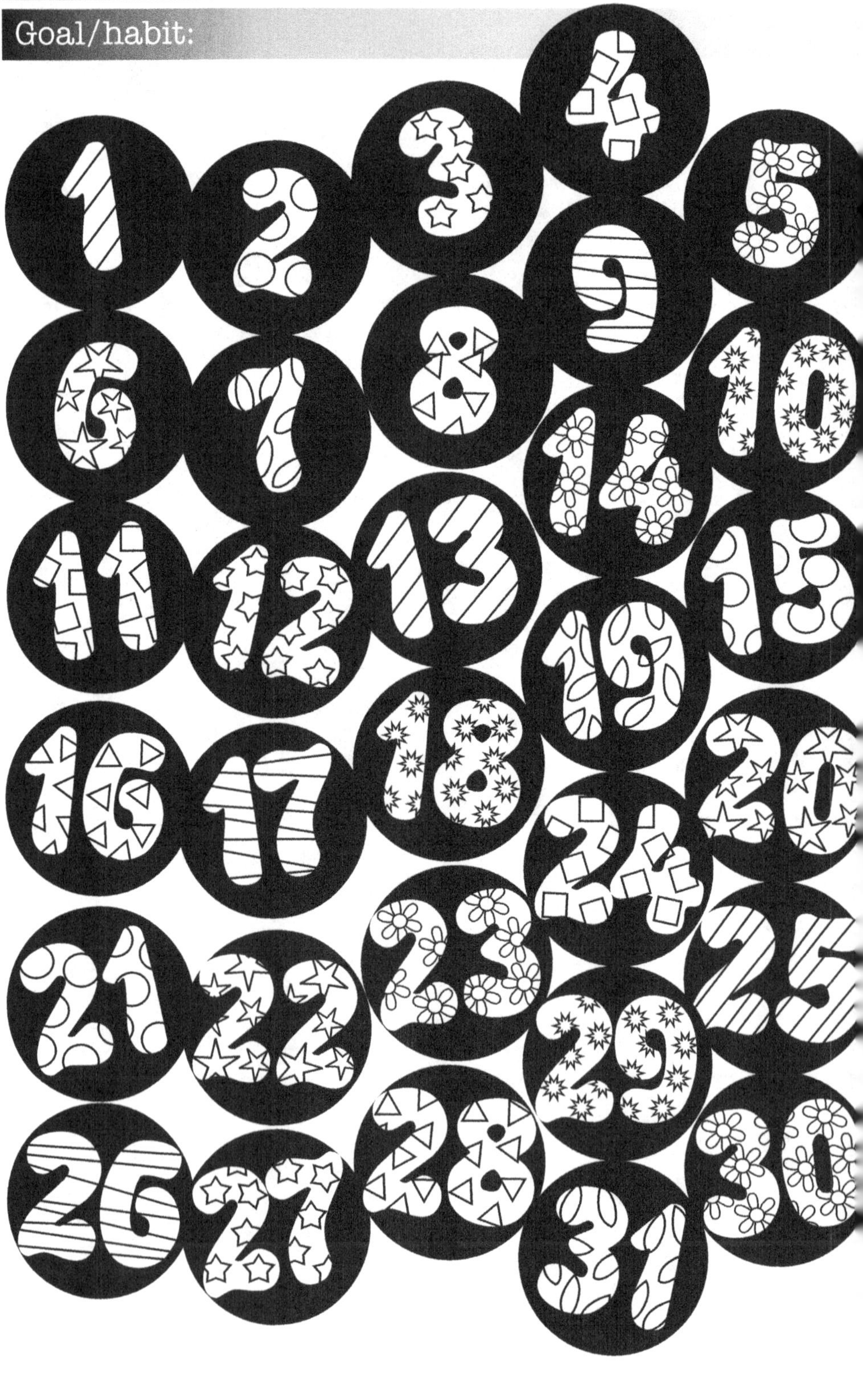

Month/year:

Goal/habit:

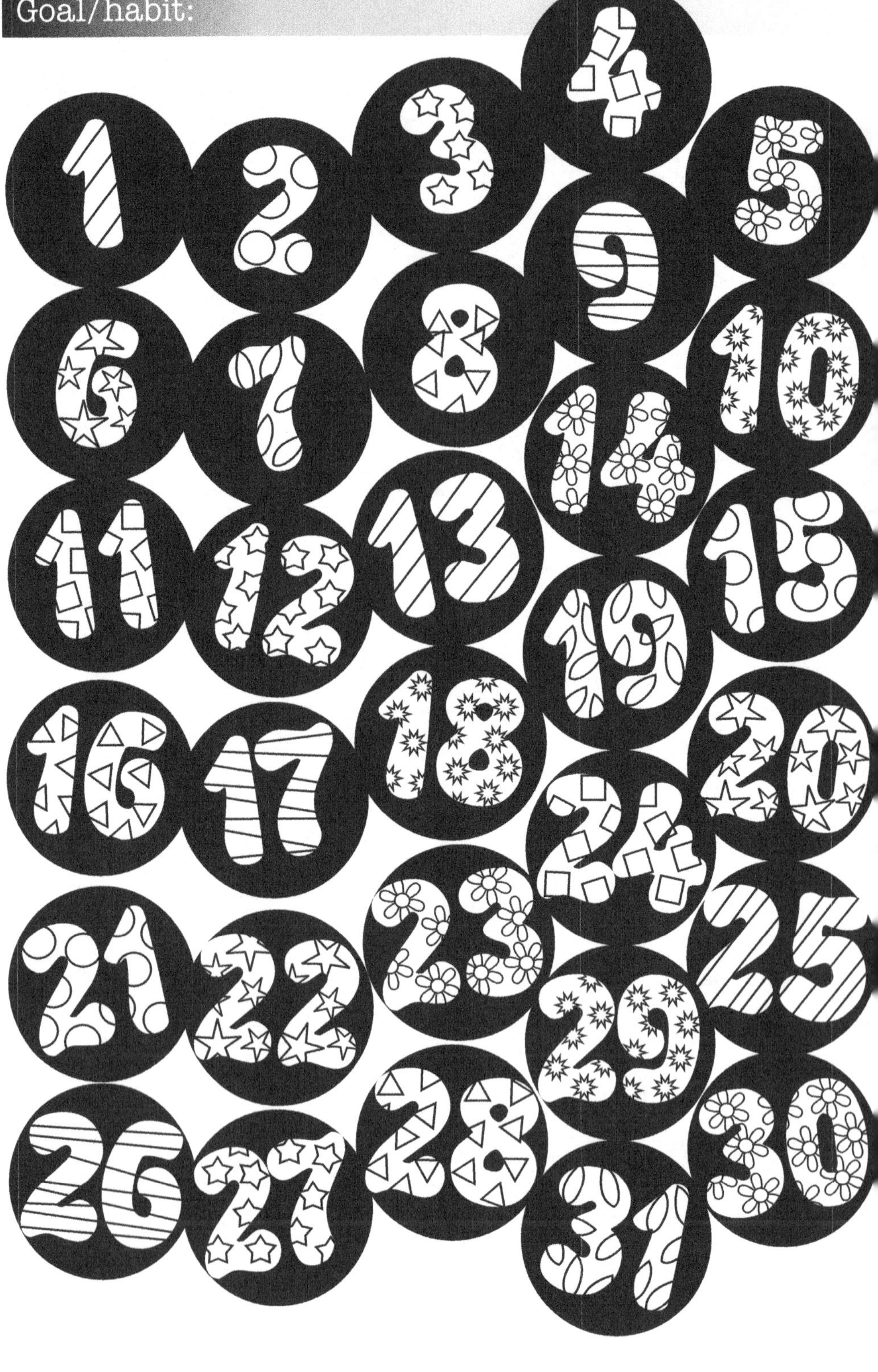

Month/year:

Goal/habit:

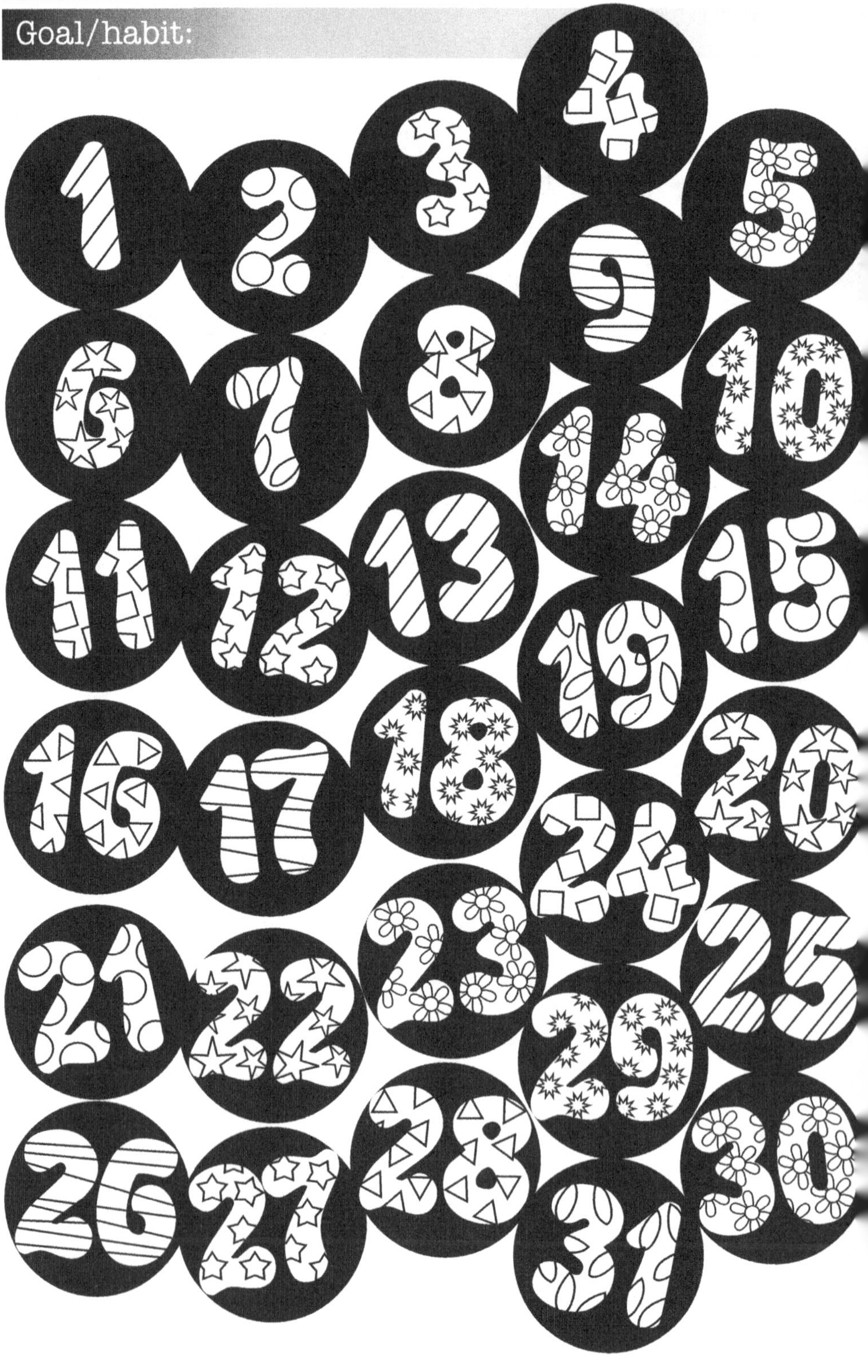

Month/year:

Goal/habit:

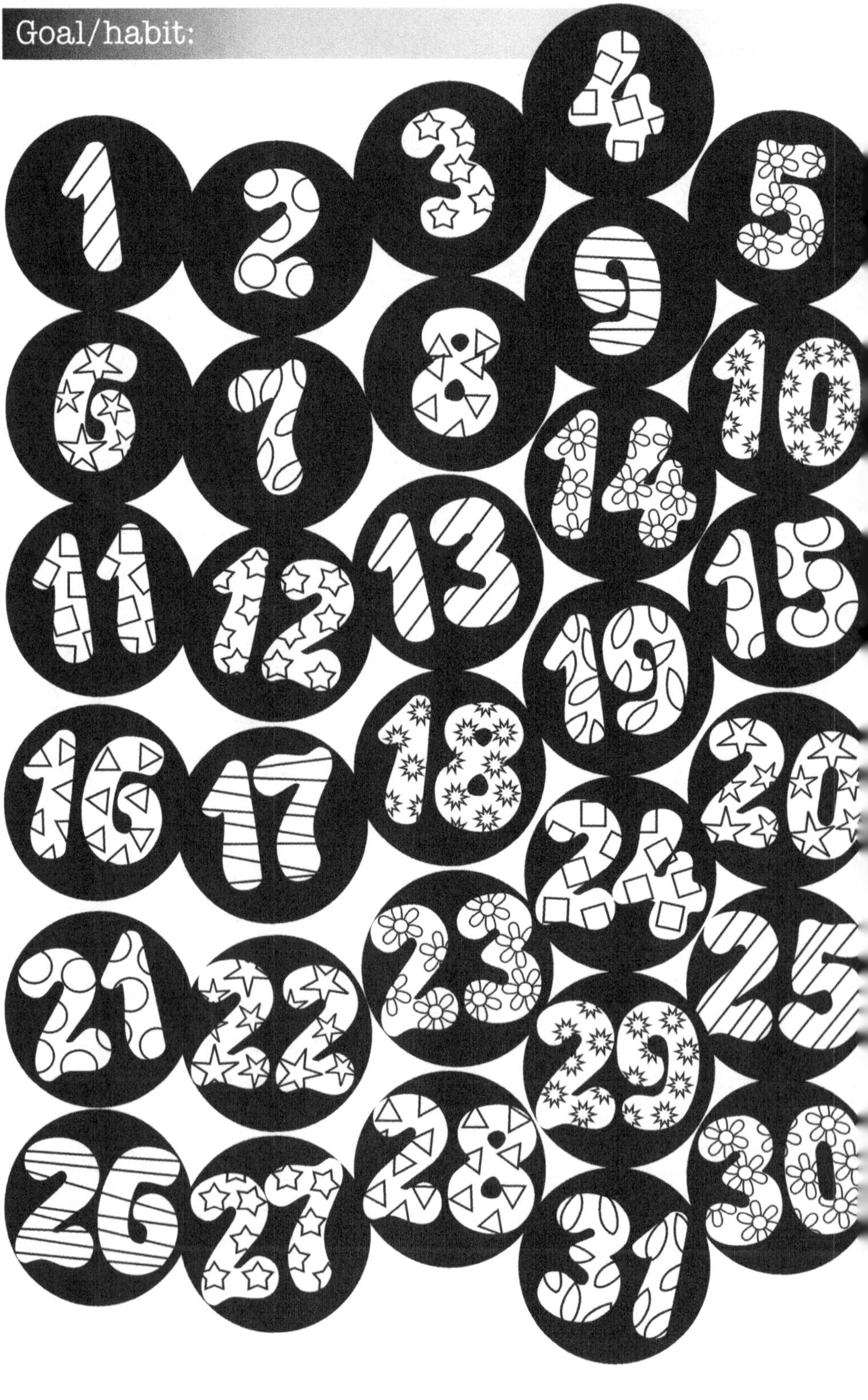

Month/year:

Goal/habit:

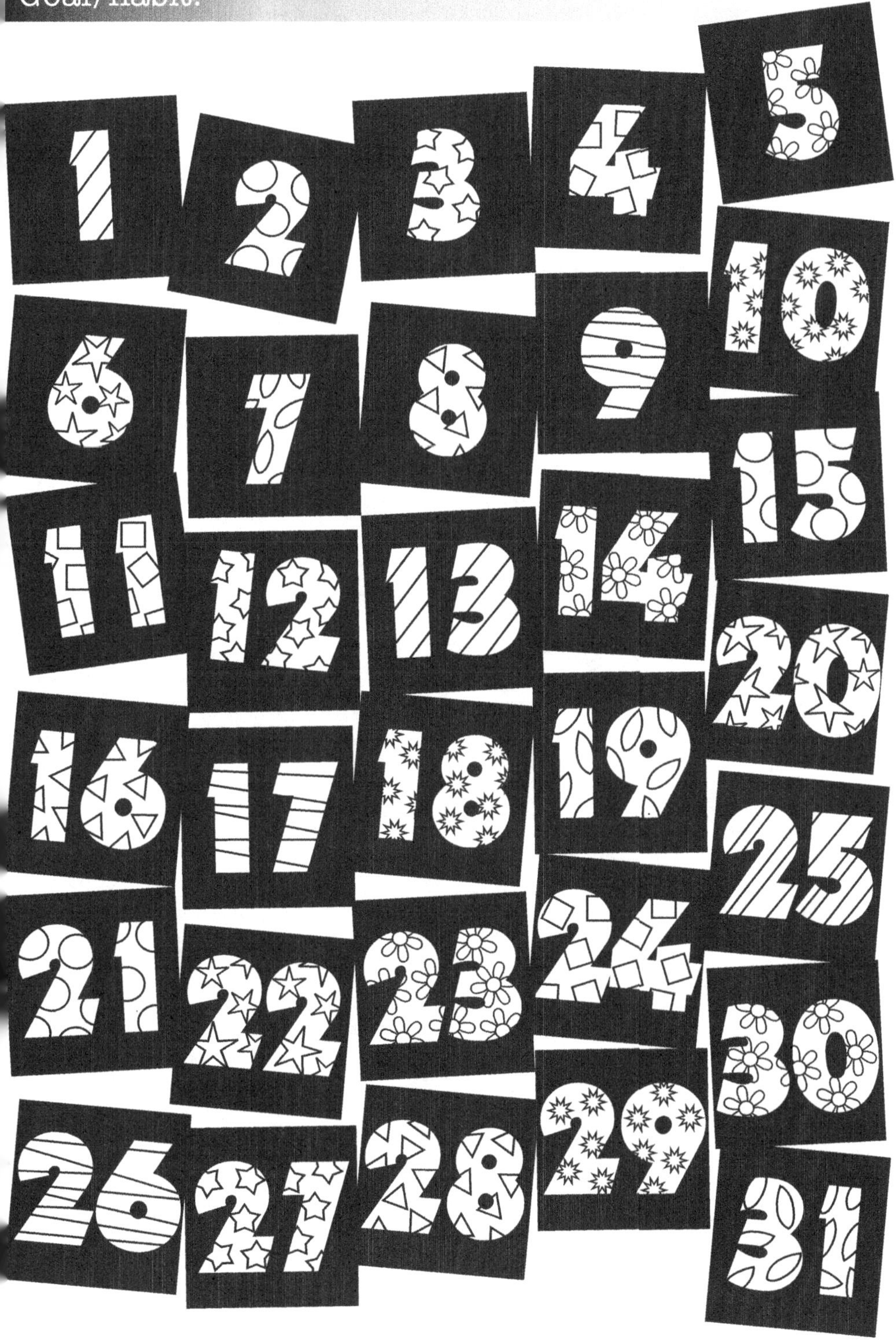

Month/year:

Goal/habit:

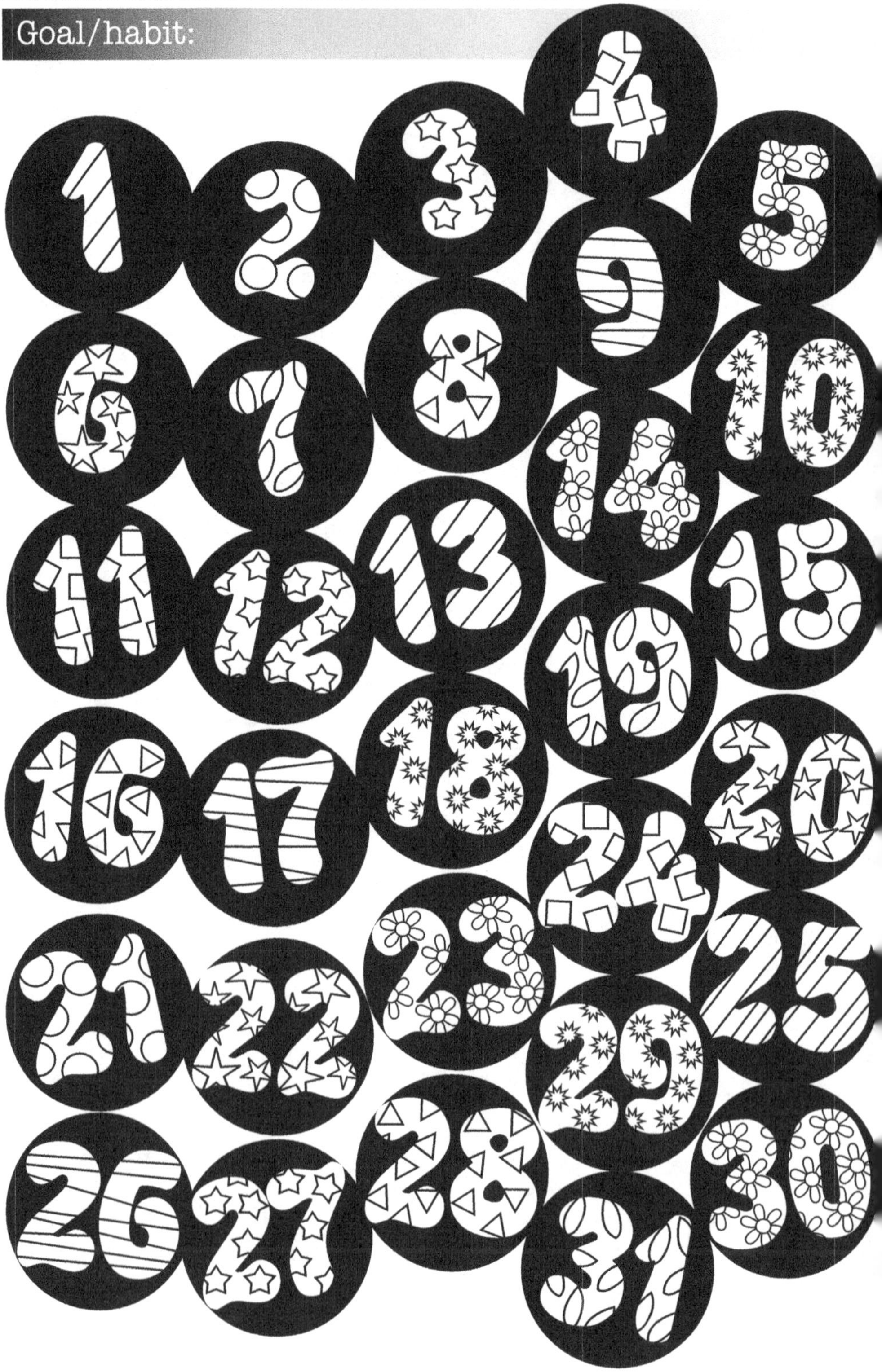

Month/year:

Goal/habit:

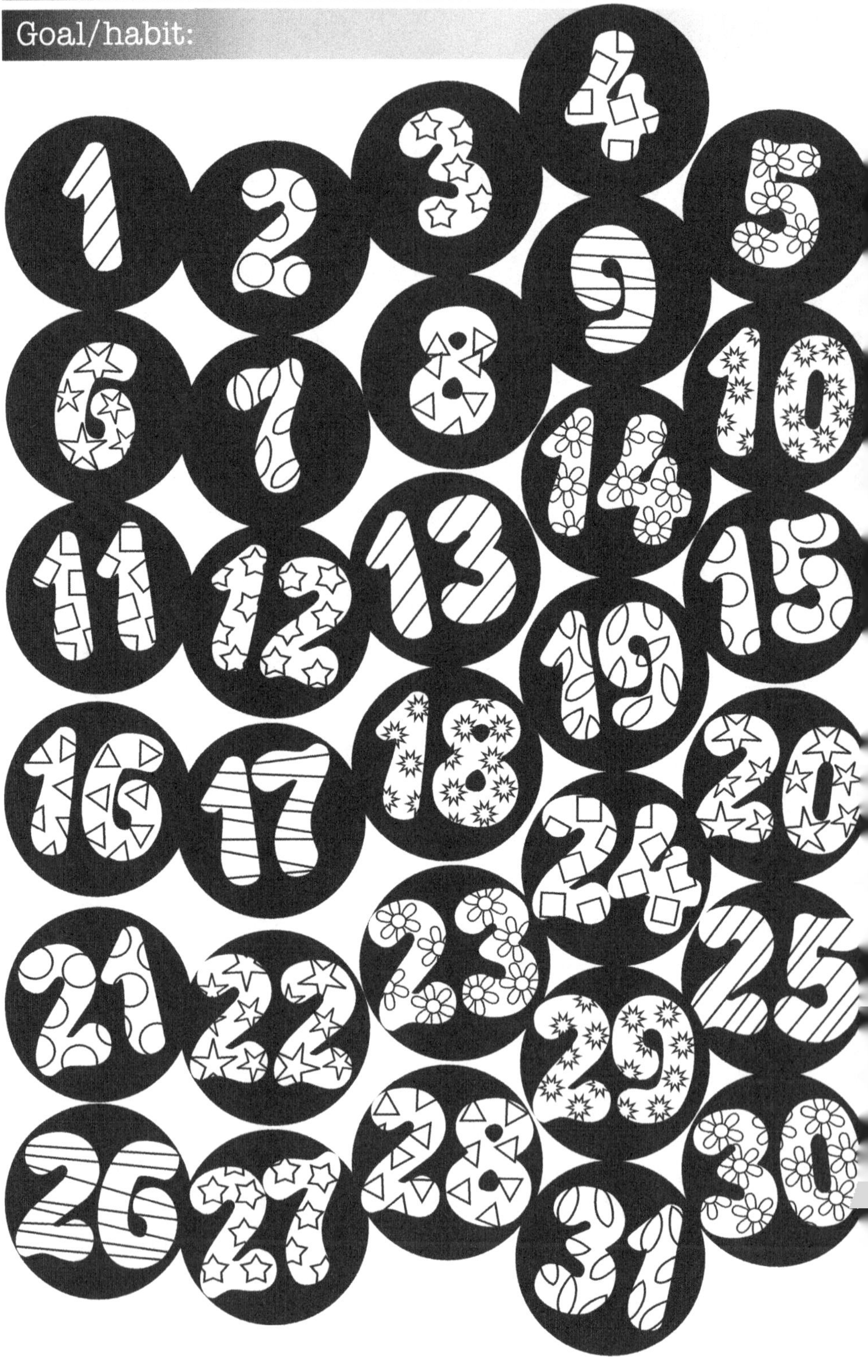

Month/year:

Goal/habit:

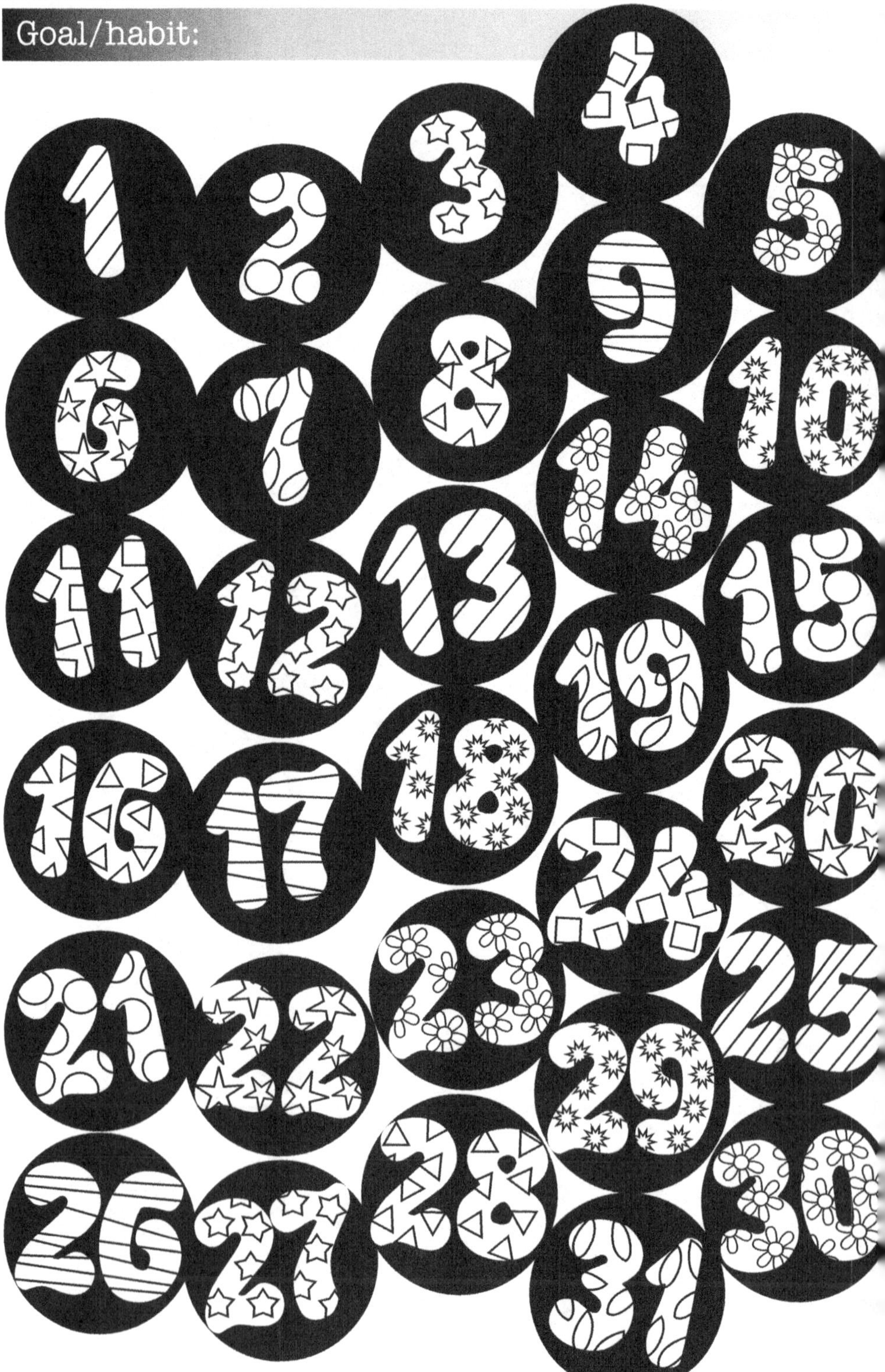

Month/year:

Goal/habit:

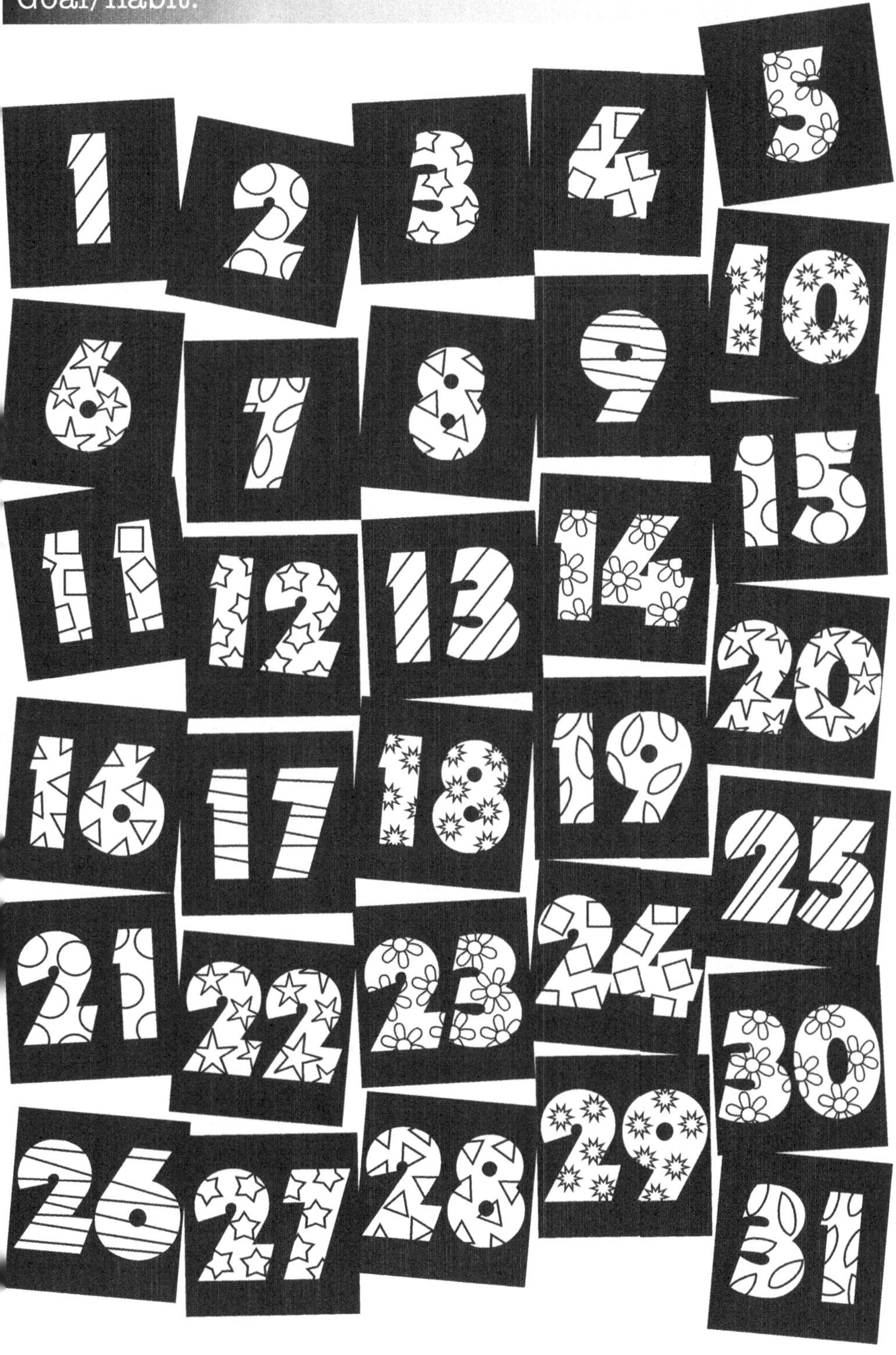

Month/year:

Goal/habit:

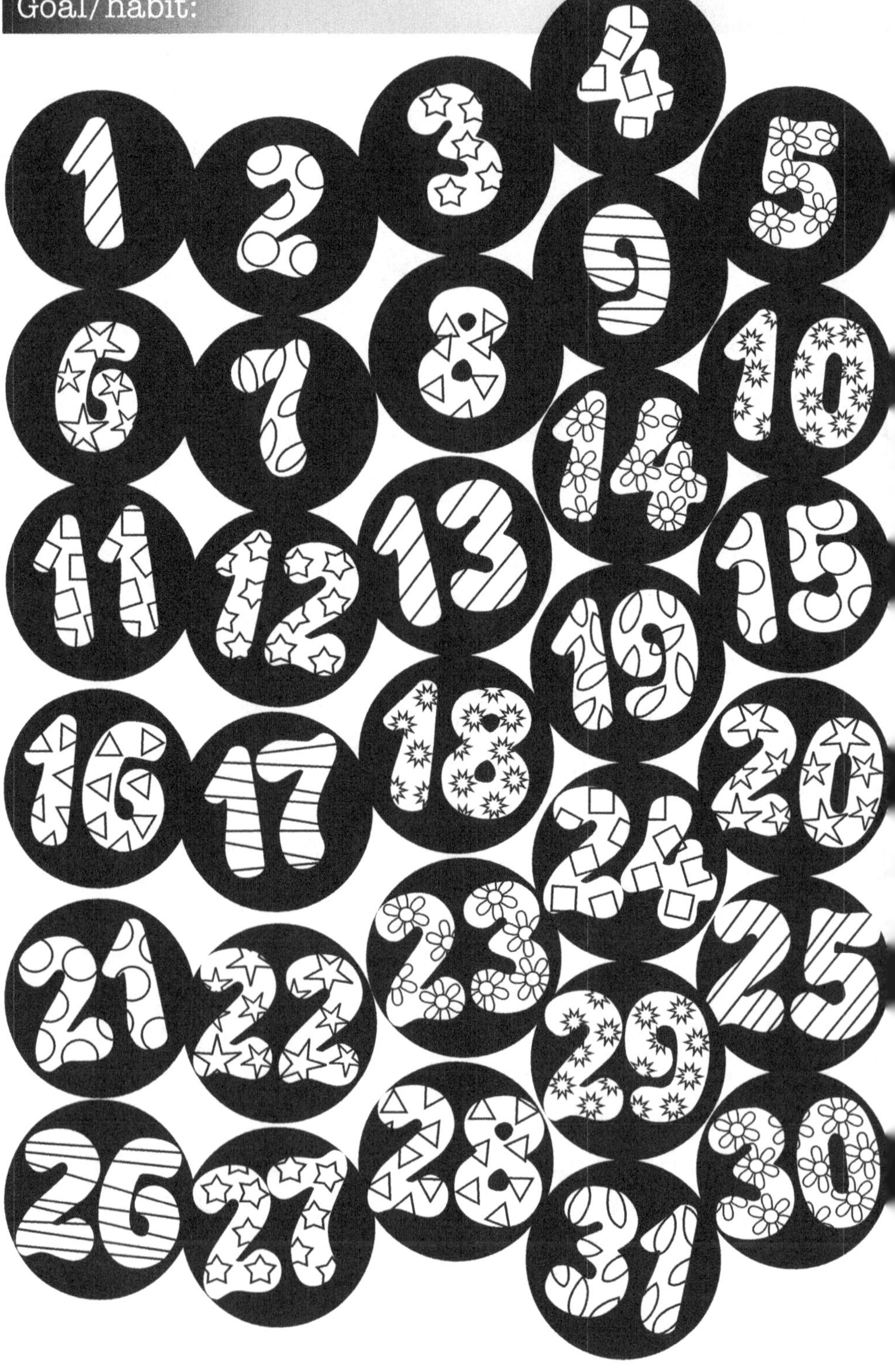

Month/year:

Goal/habit:

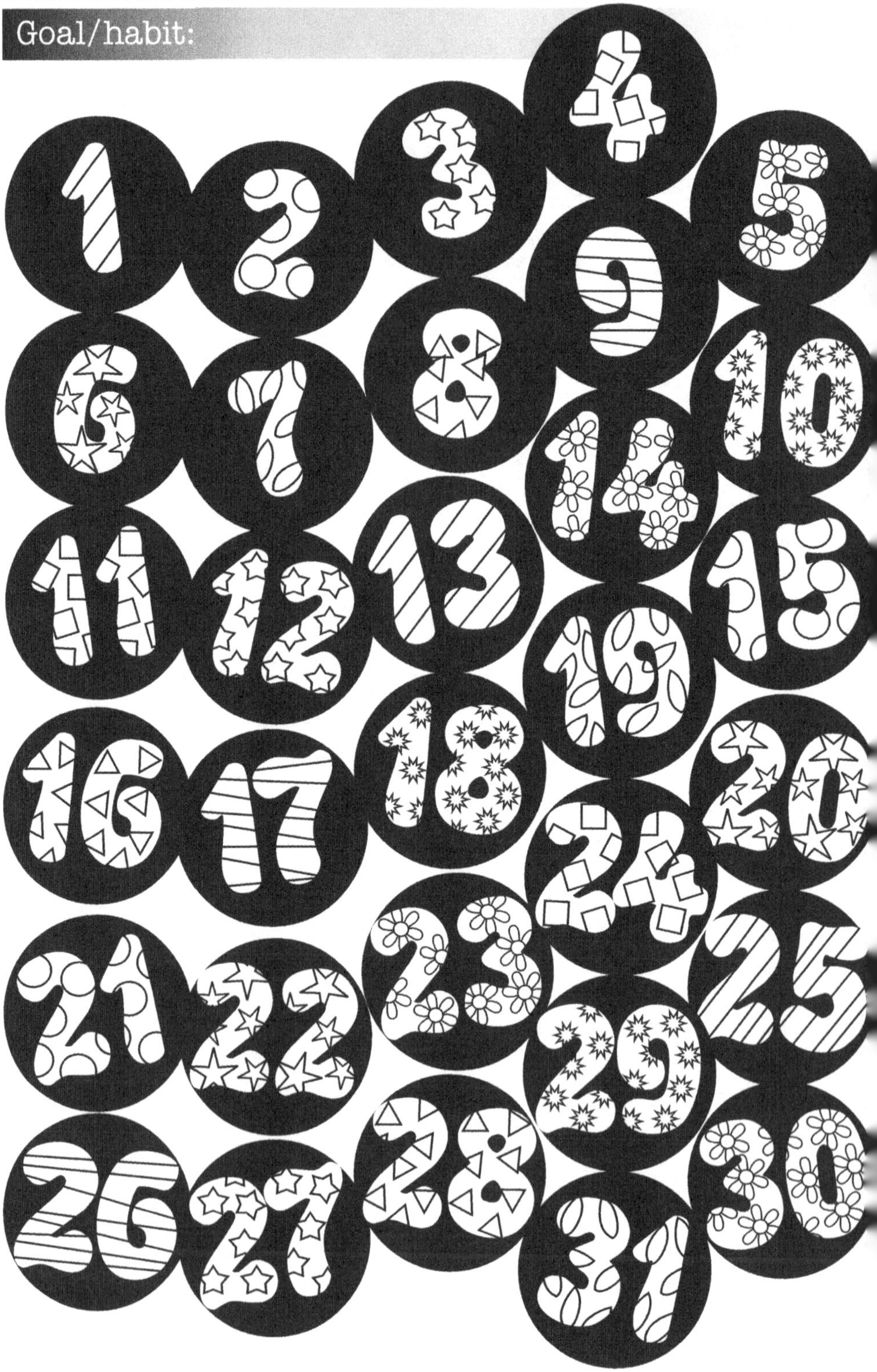

Month/year:

Goal/habit:

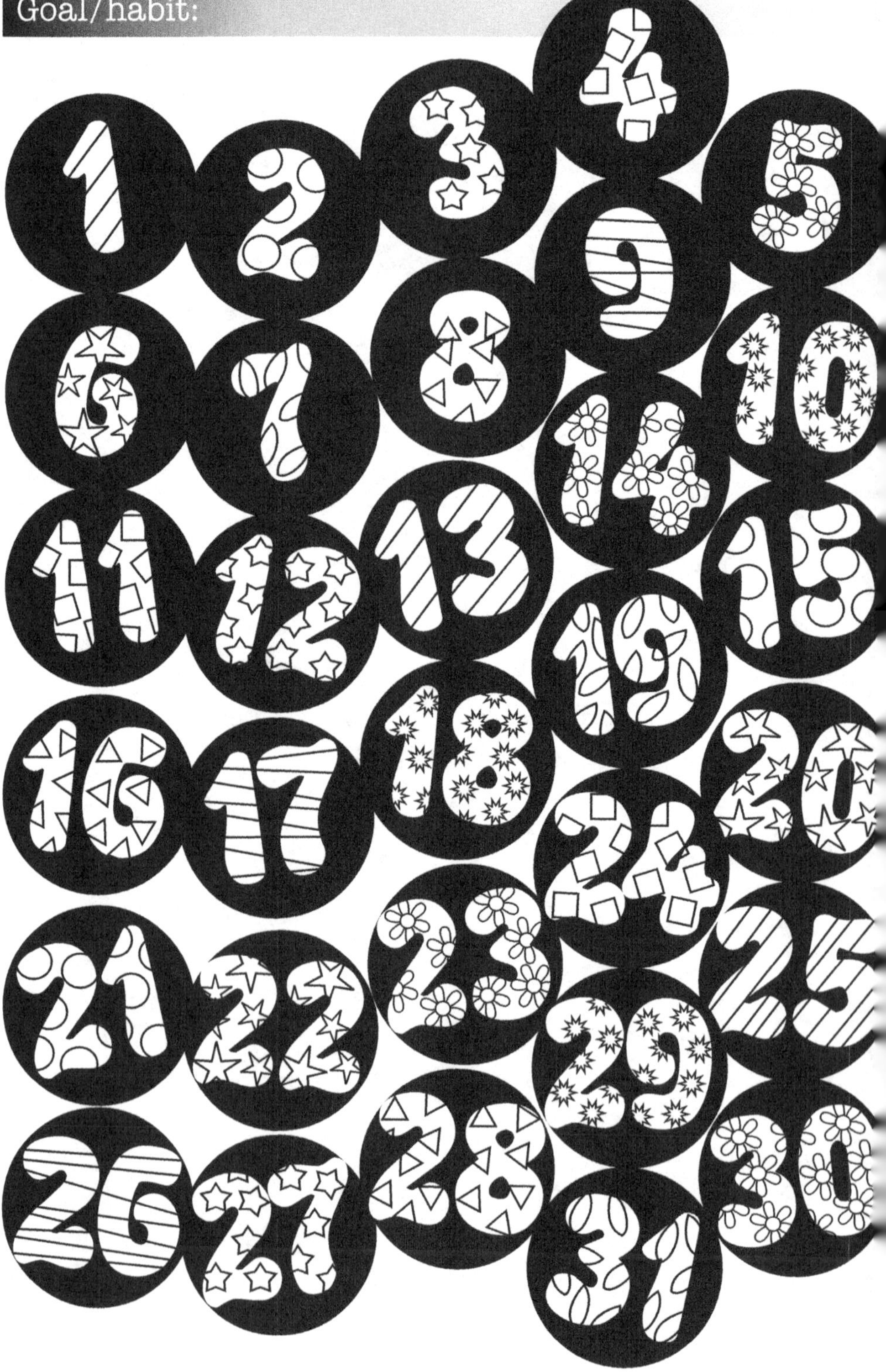

Month/year:

Goal/habit:

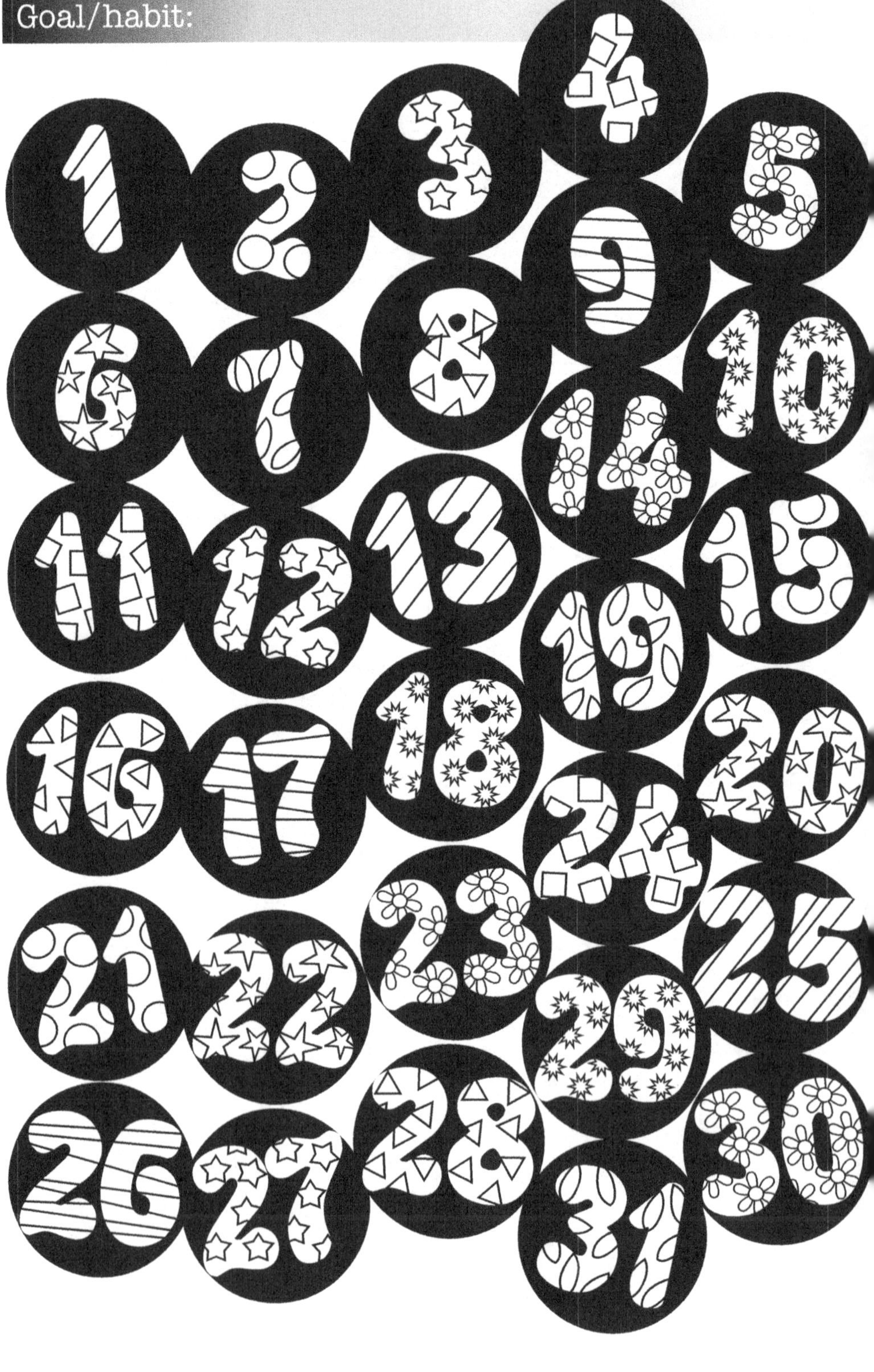

Month/year:

Goal/habit:

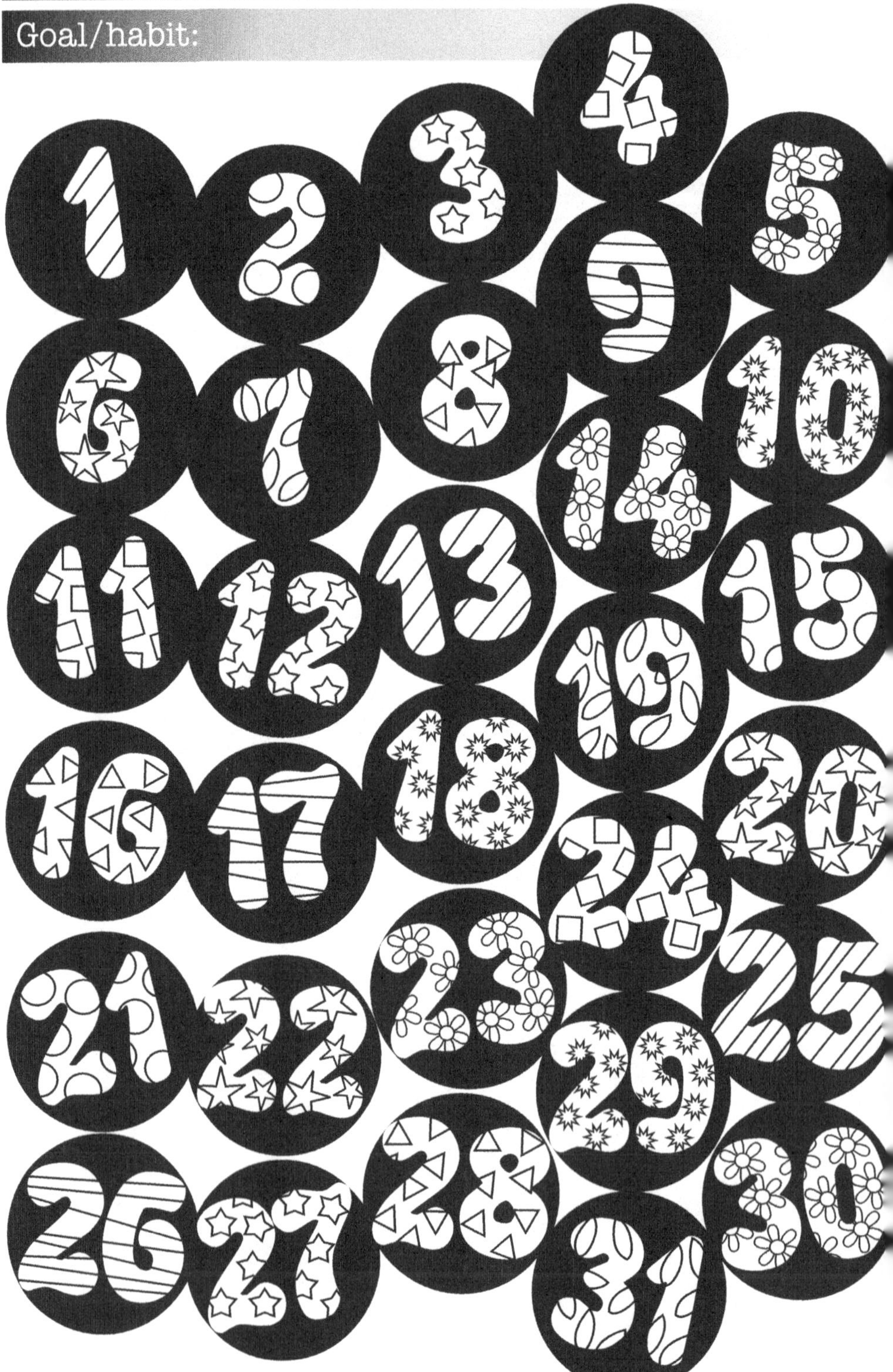

Month/year:

Goal/habit:

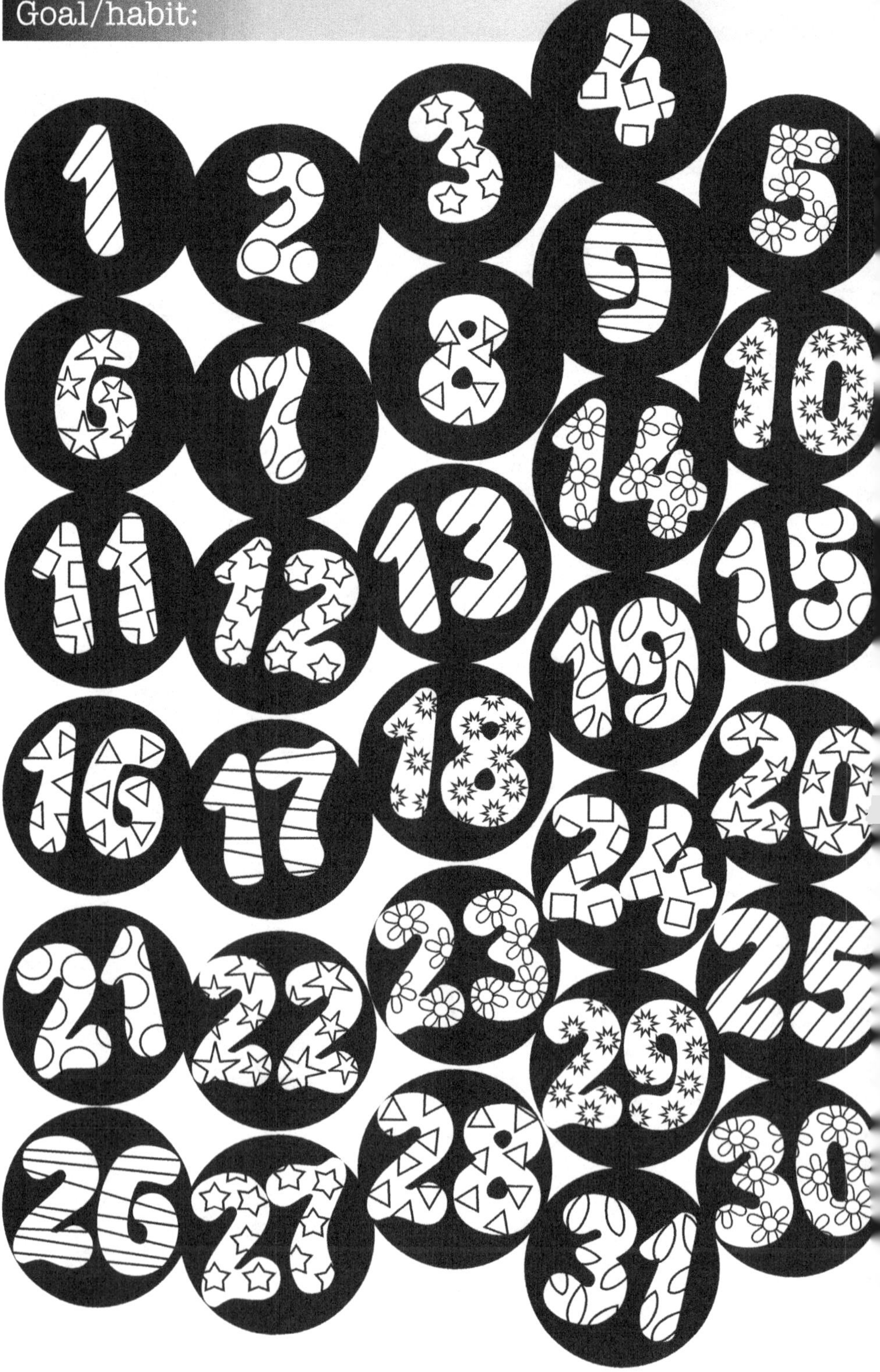

Month/year:

Goal/habit:

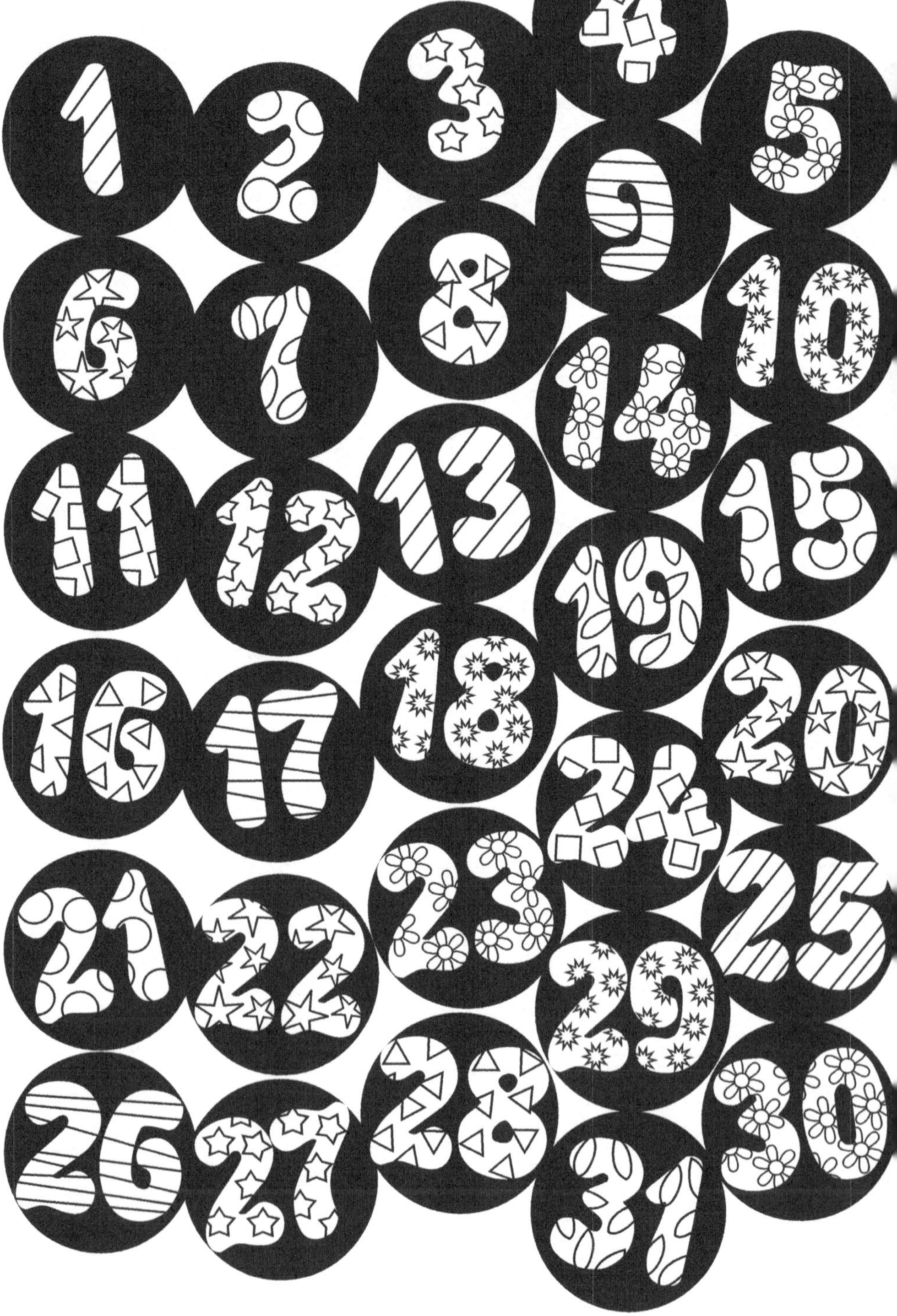

Month/year:

Goal/habit:

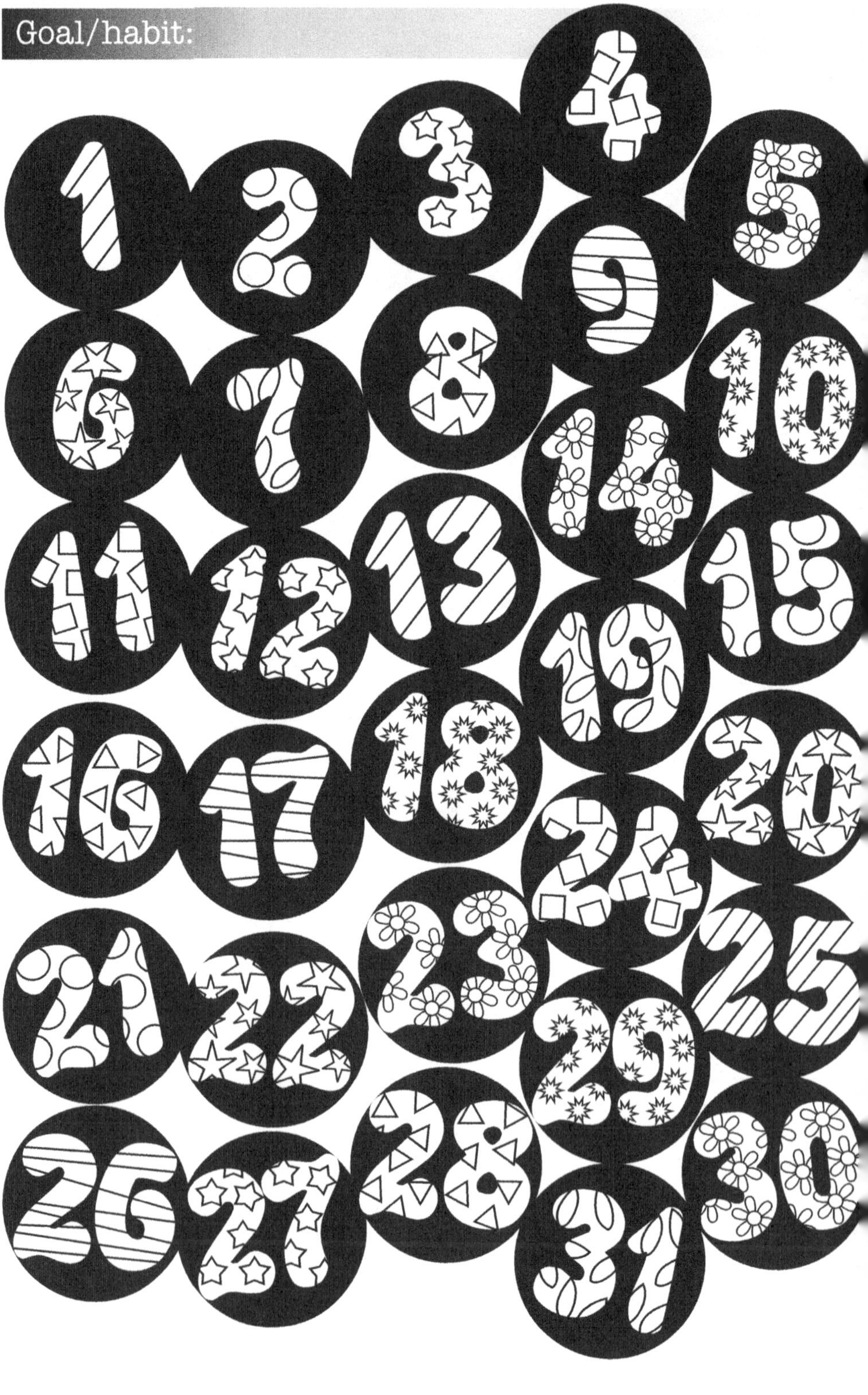

Month/year:

Goal/habit:

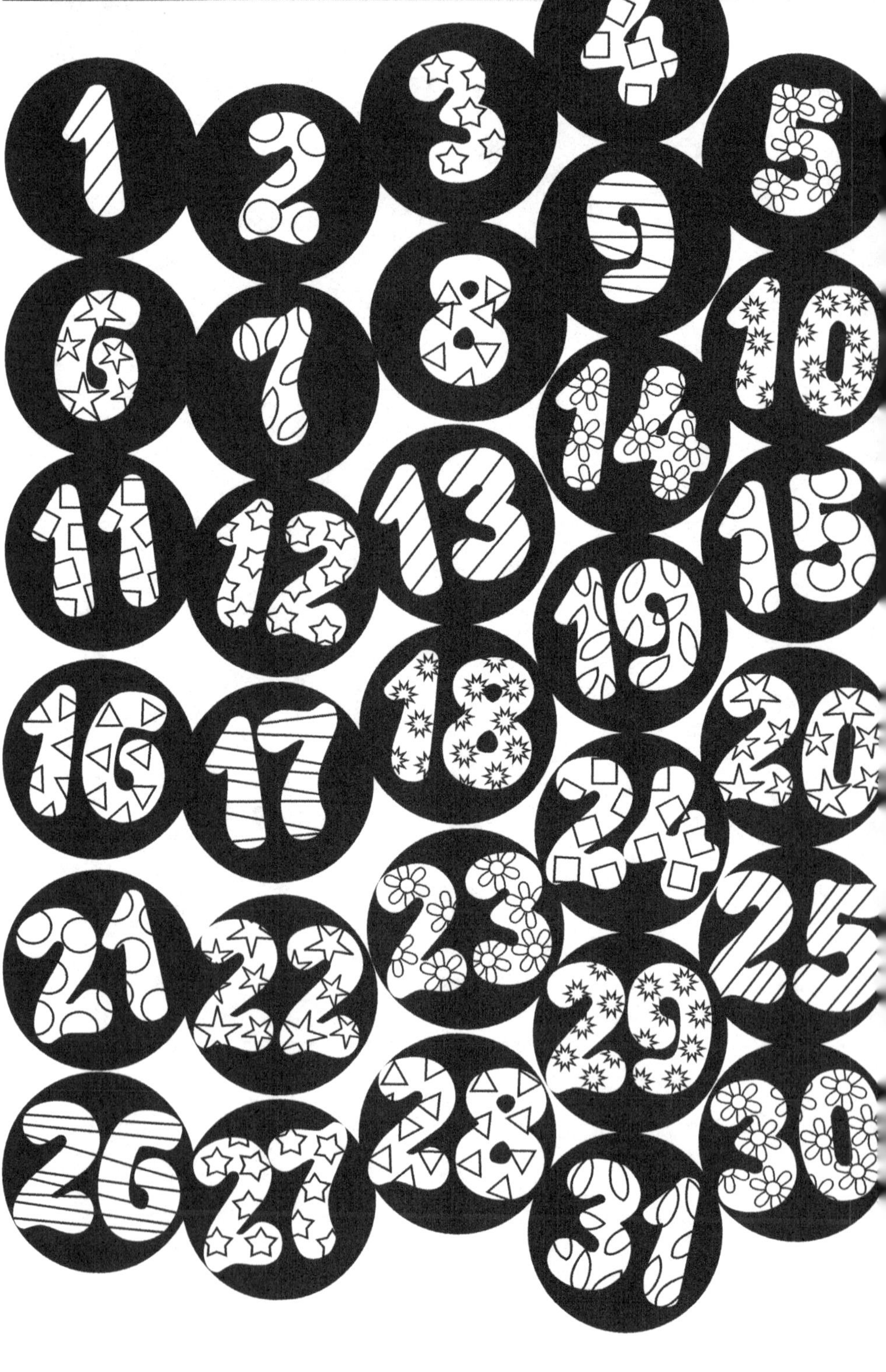

1 2 3 4 5
6 7 8 9 10
11 12 13 14 15
16 17 18 19 20
21 22 23 24 25
26 27 28 29 30
31

Month/year:

Goal/habit:

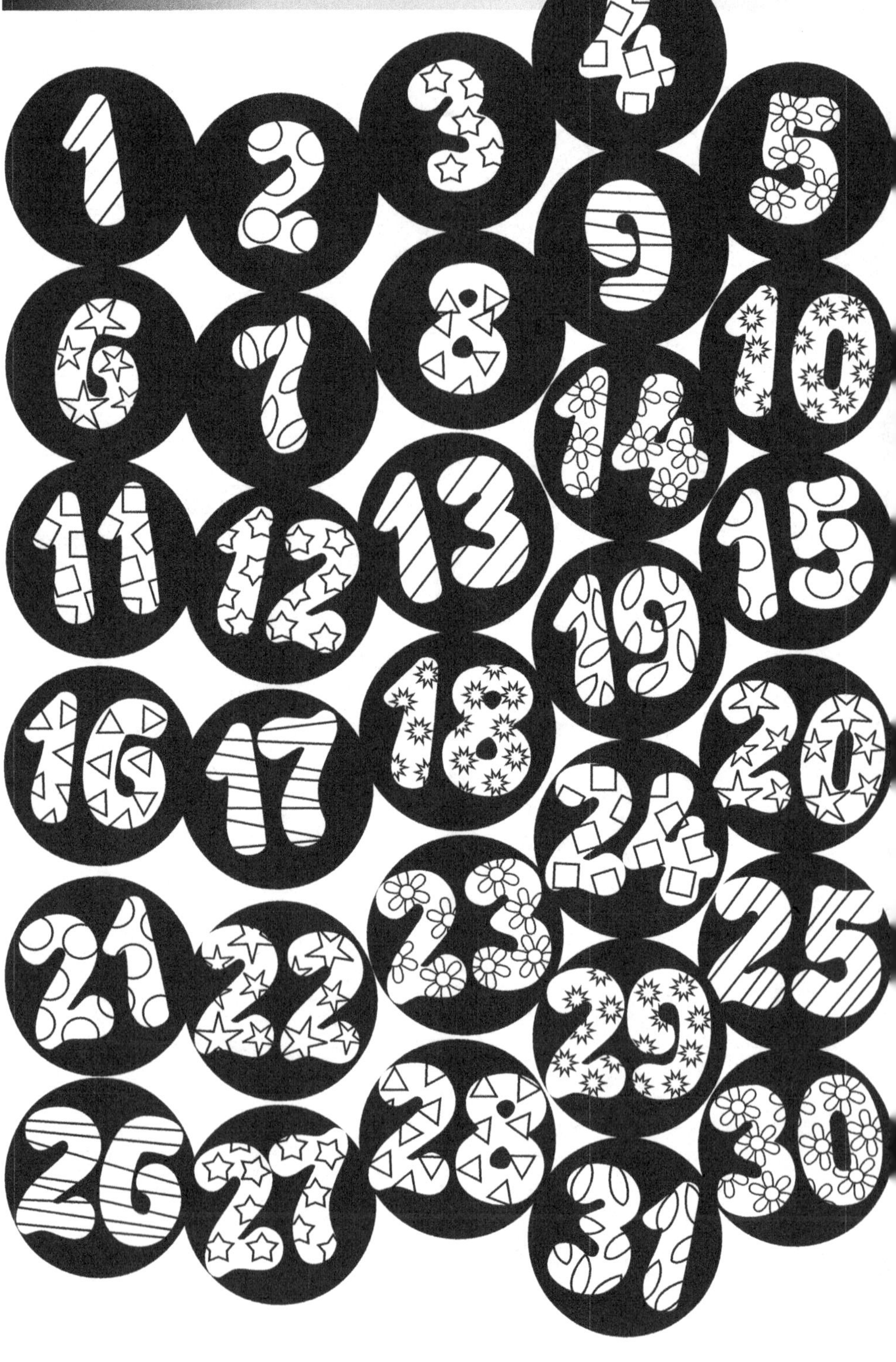

Month/year:

Goal/habit:

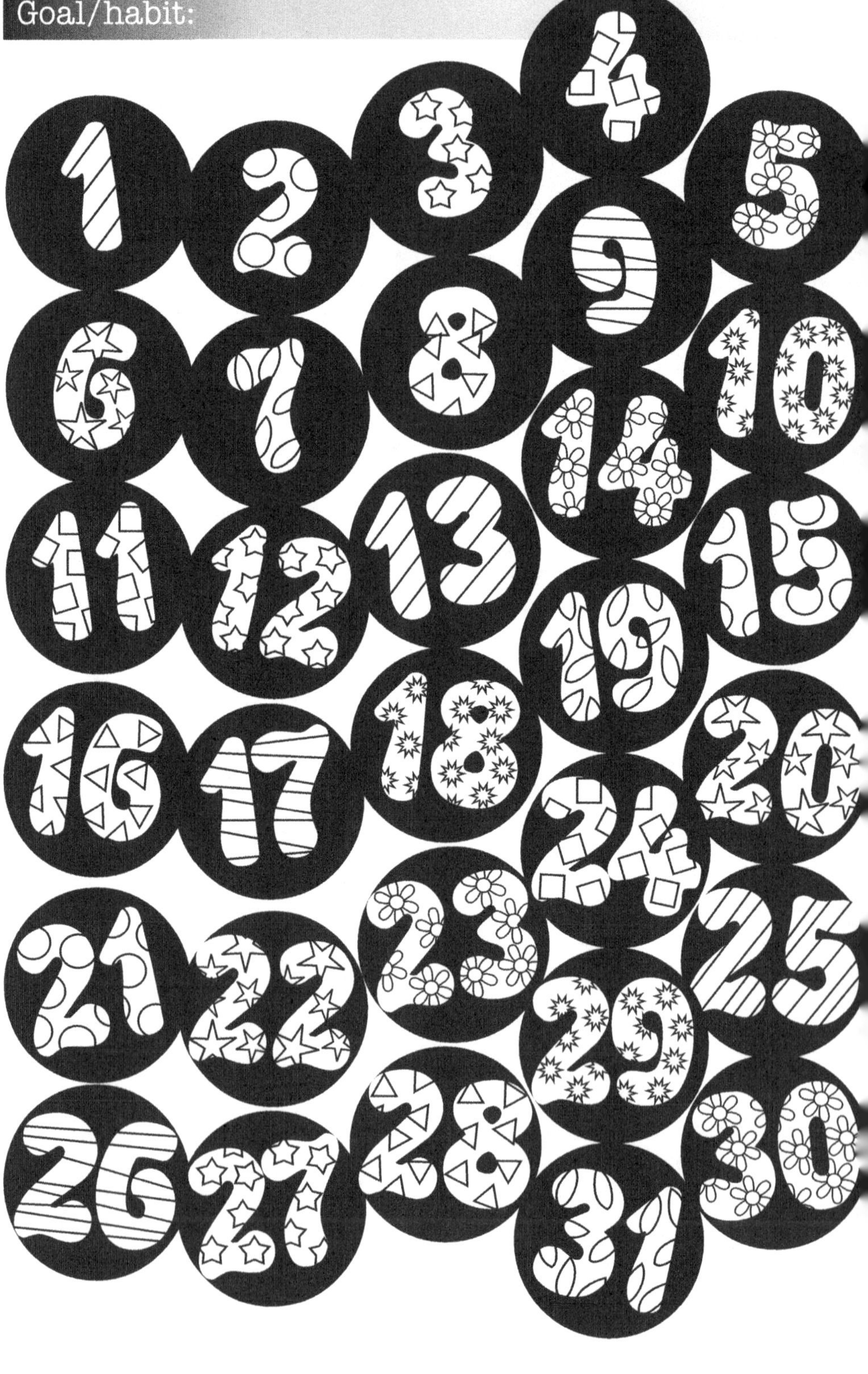

Month/year:

Goal/habit:

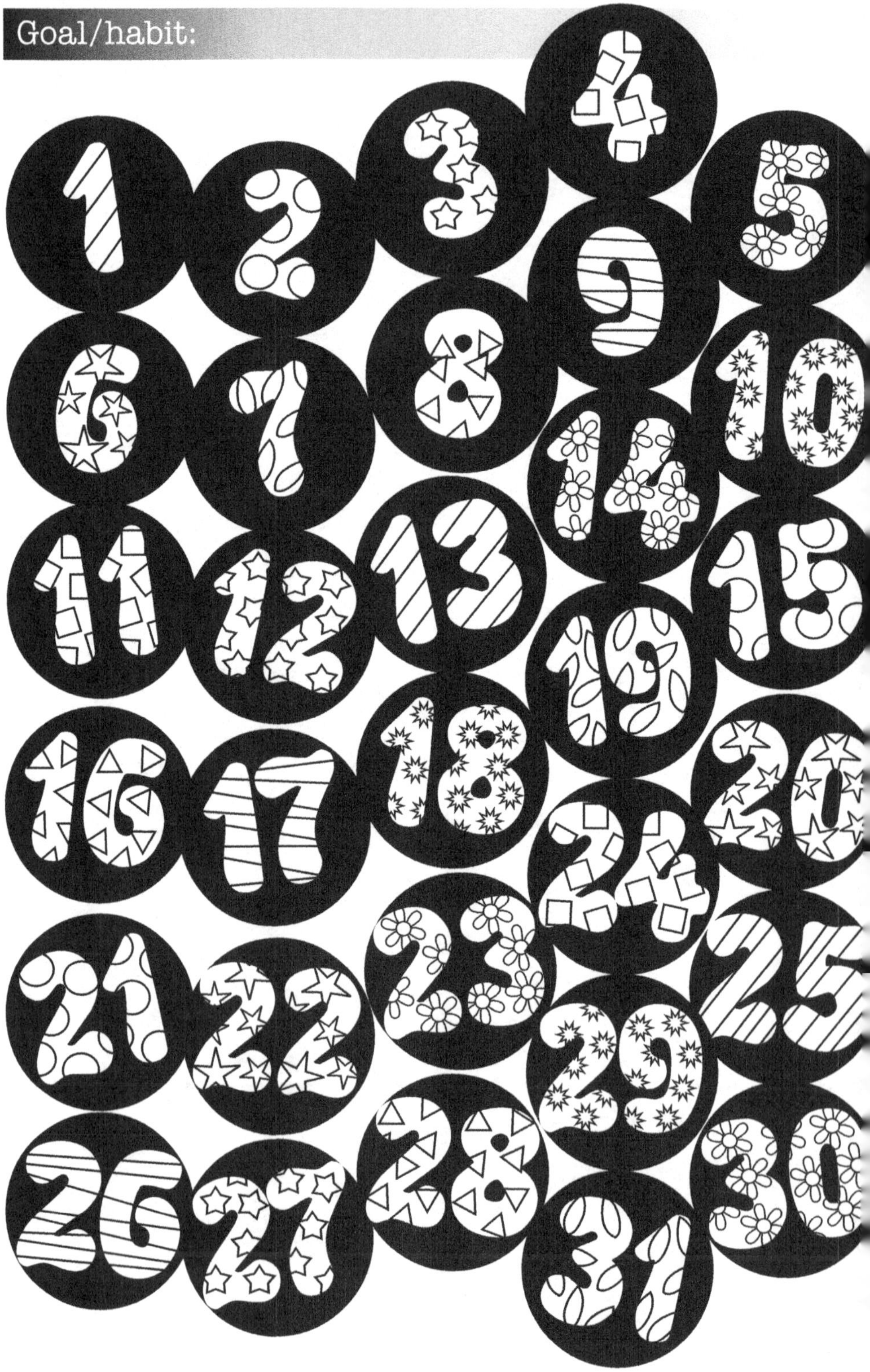

Month/year:

Goal/habit:

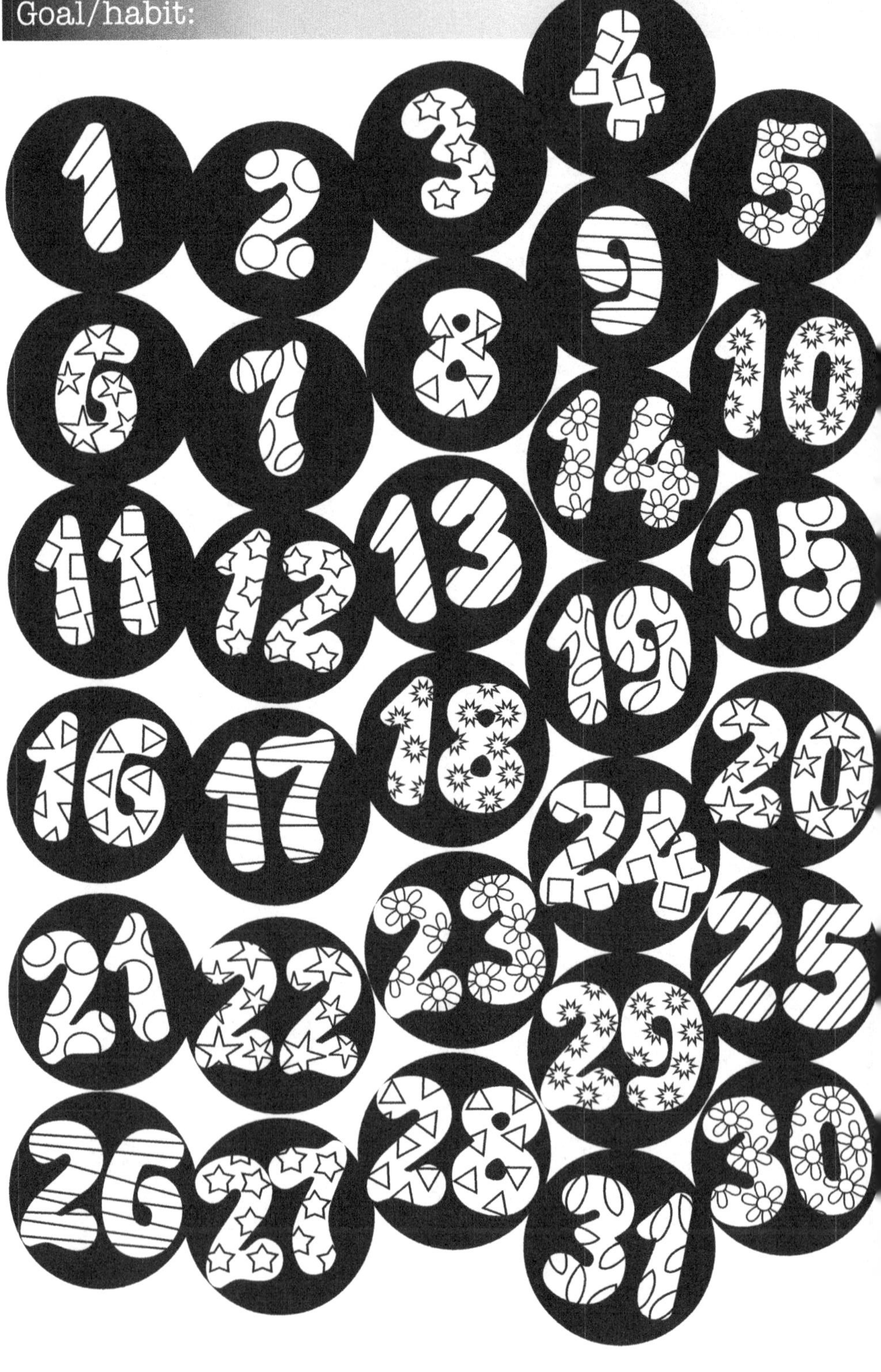

Month/year:

Goal/habit:

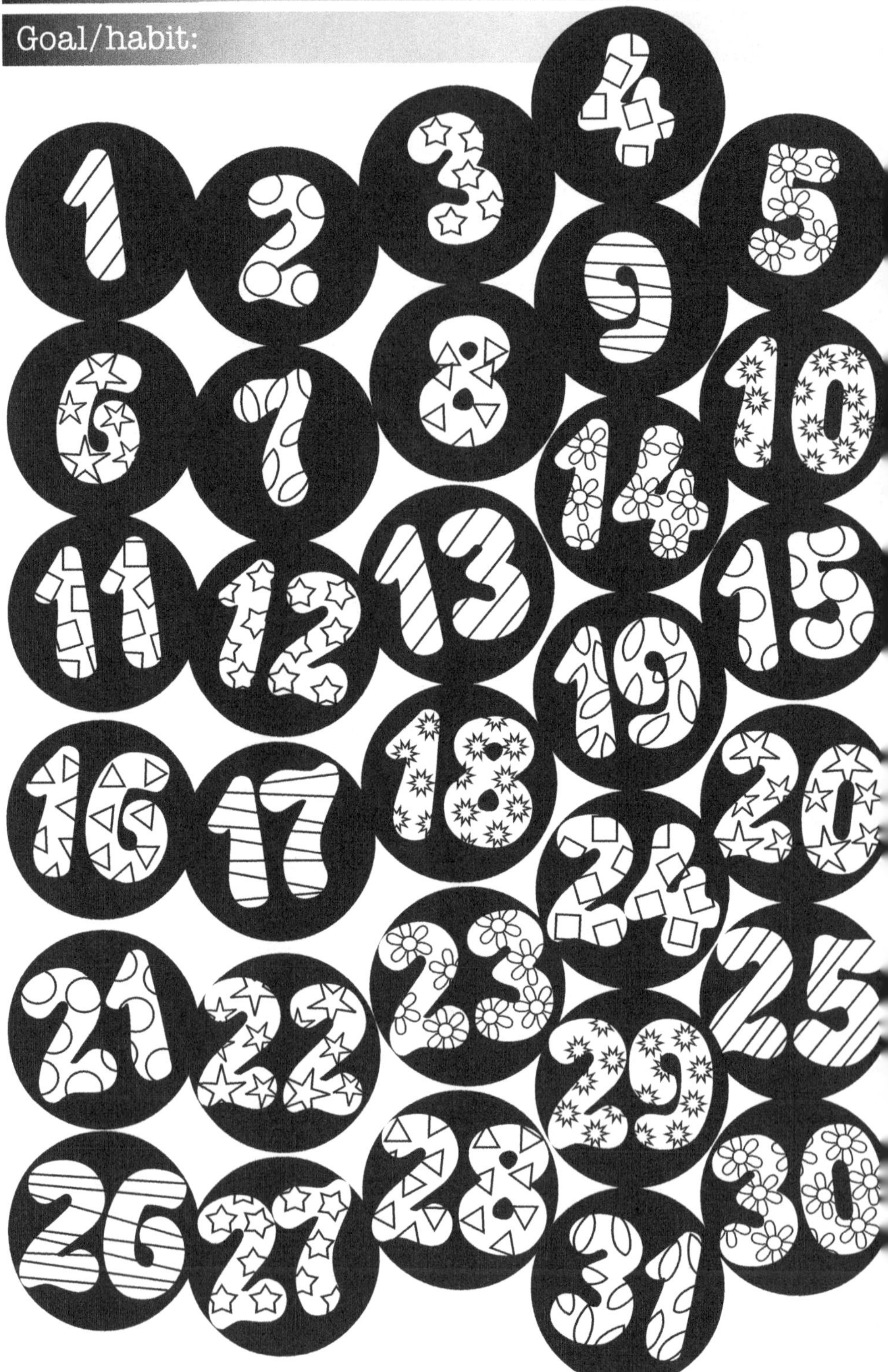

Month/year:

Goal/habit:

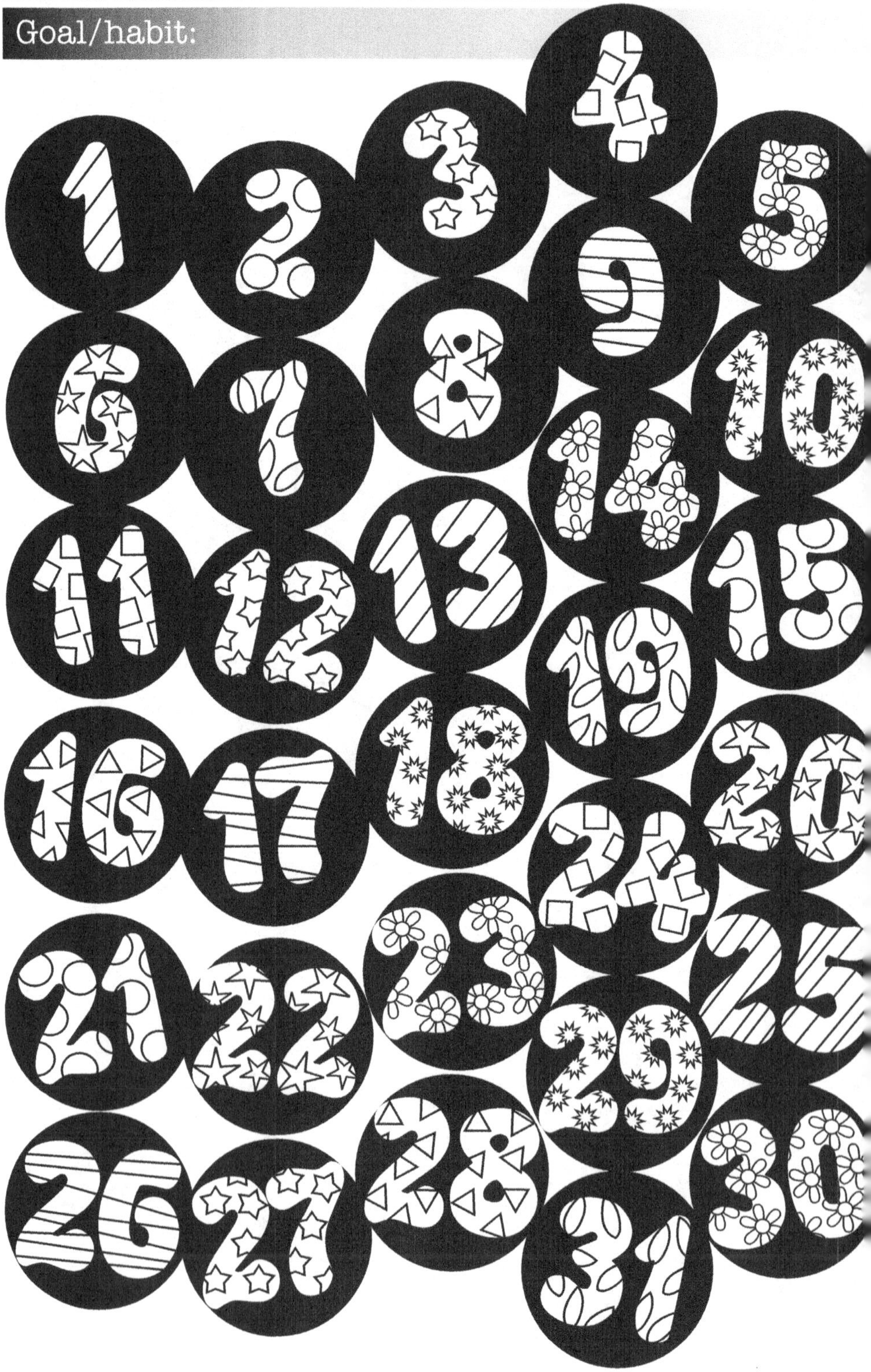

Month/year:

Goal/habit:

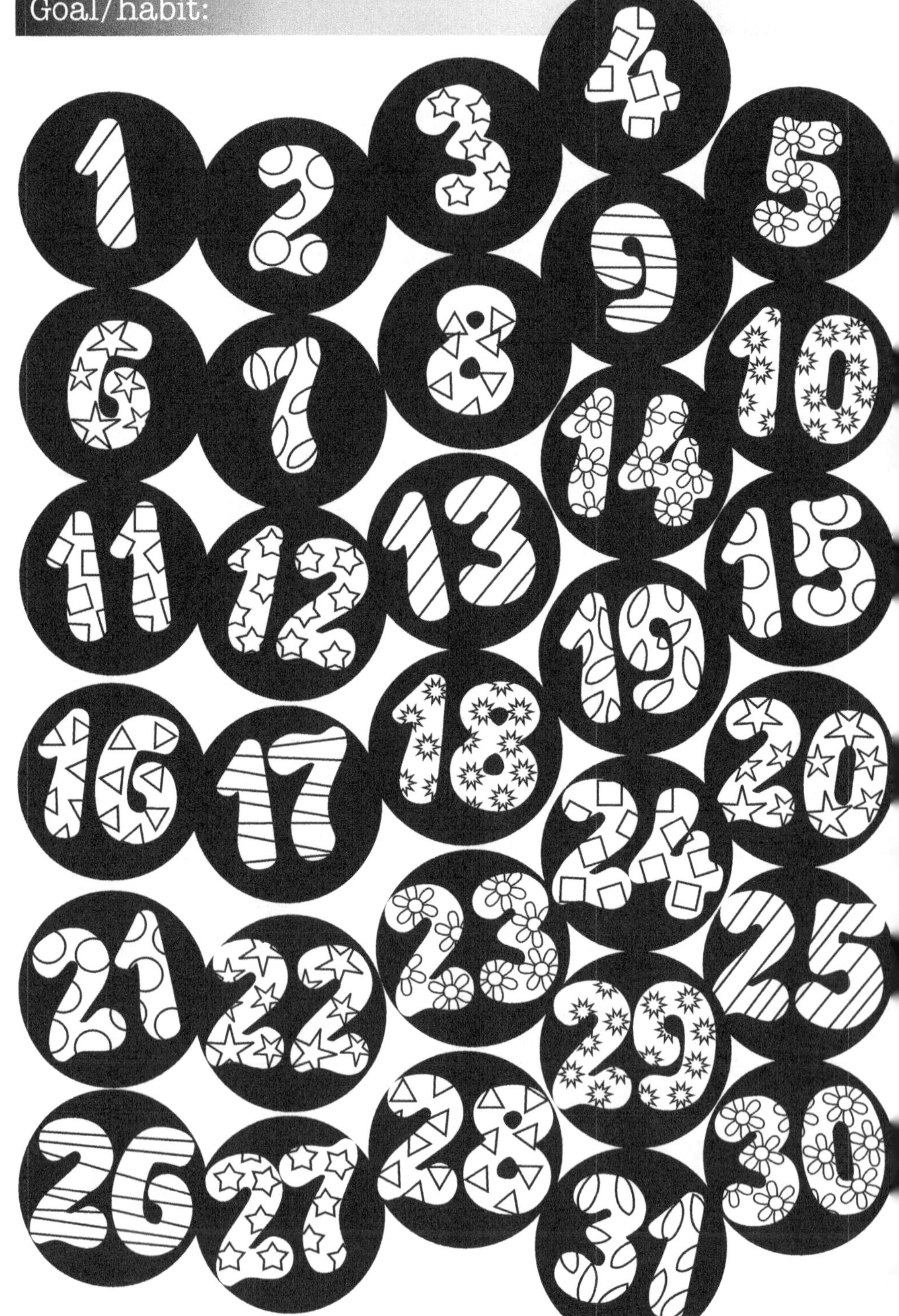

Month/year:

Goal/habit:

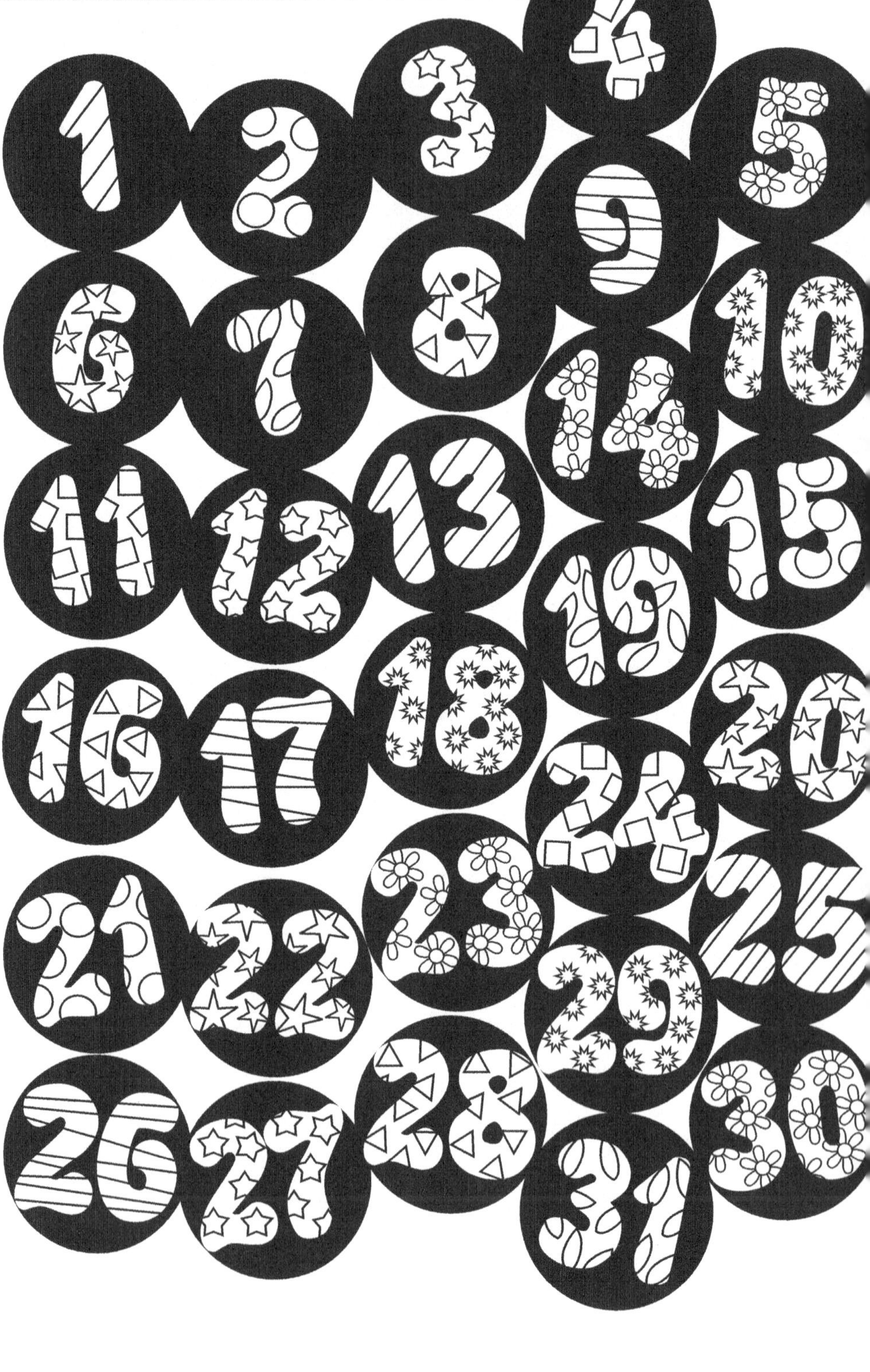

Month/year:

Goal/habit:

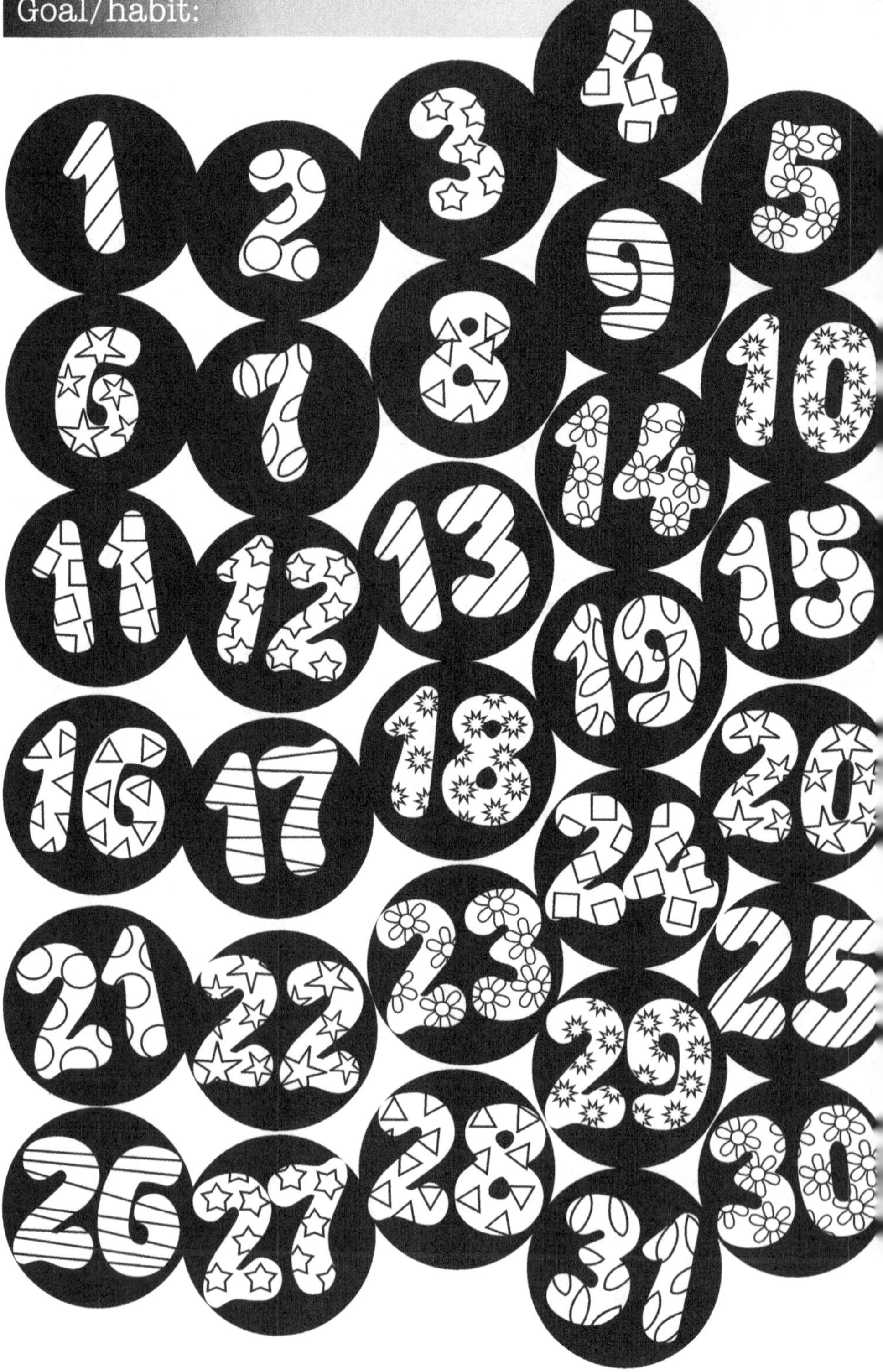

Month/year:

Goal/habit:

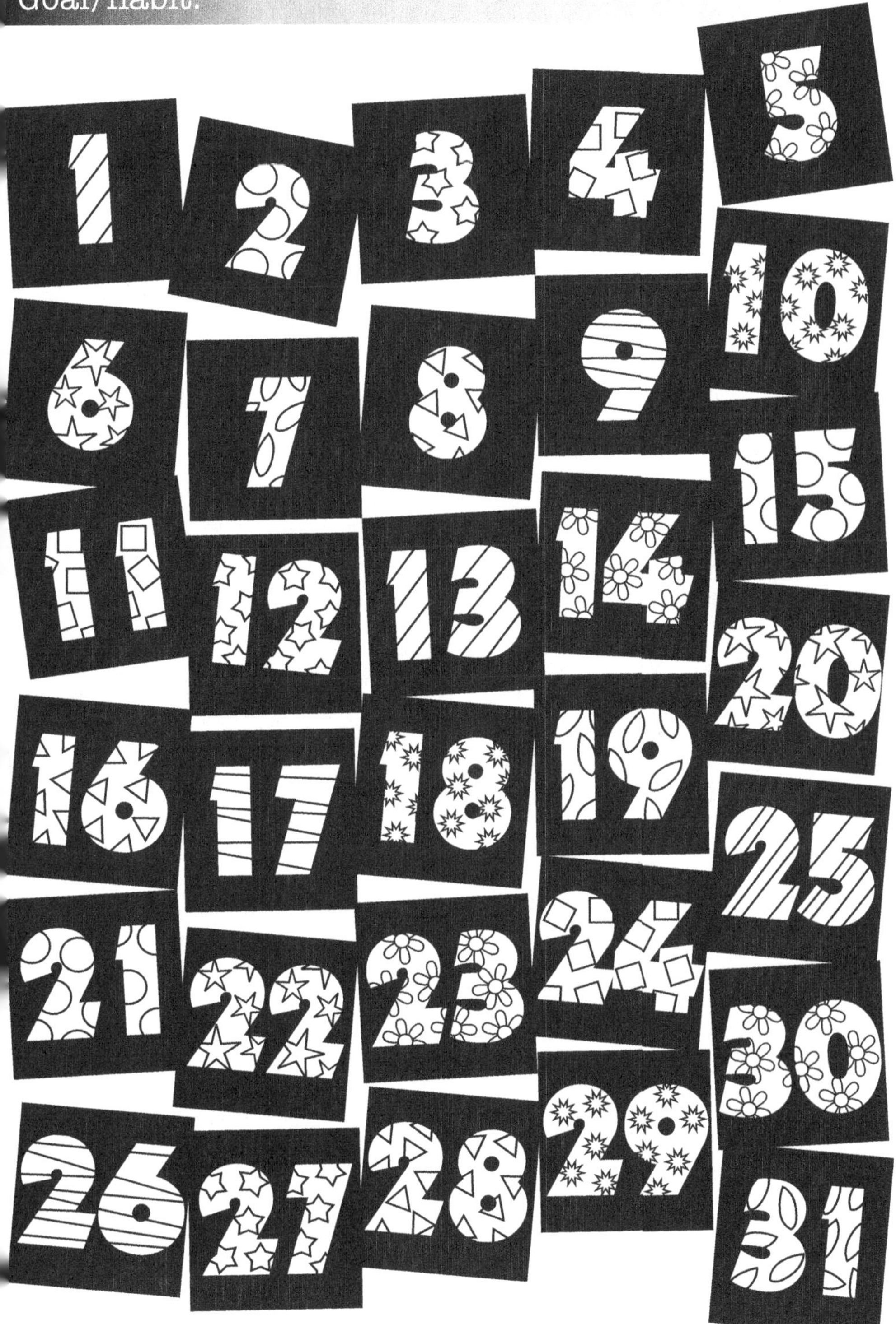

Month/year:

Goal/habit:

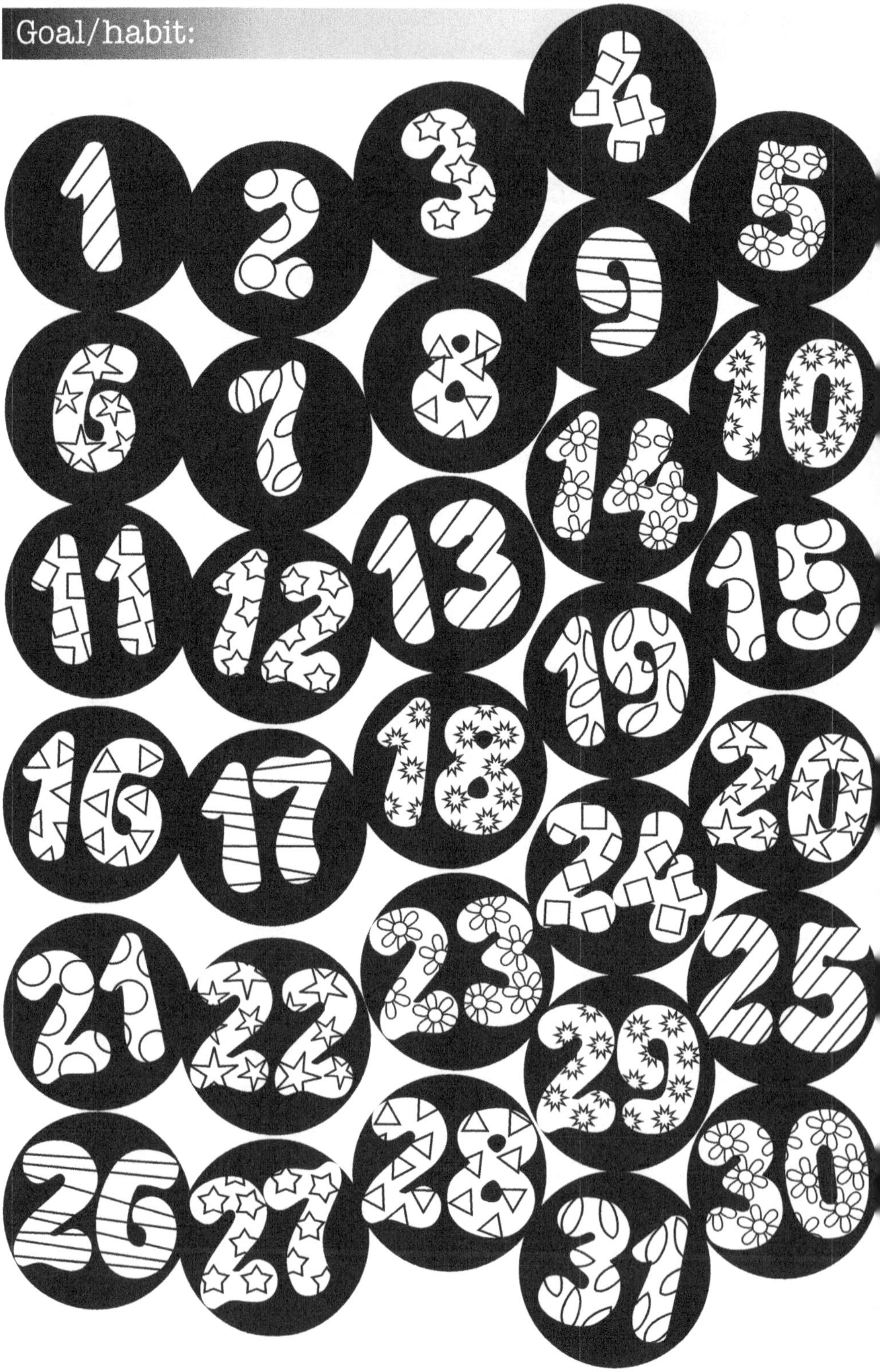

Month/year:

Goal/habit:

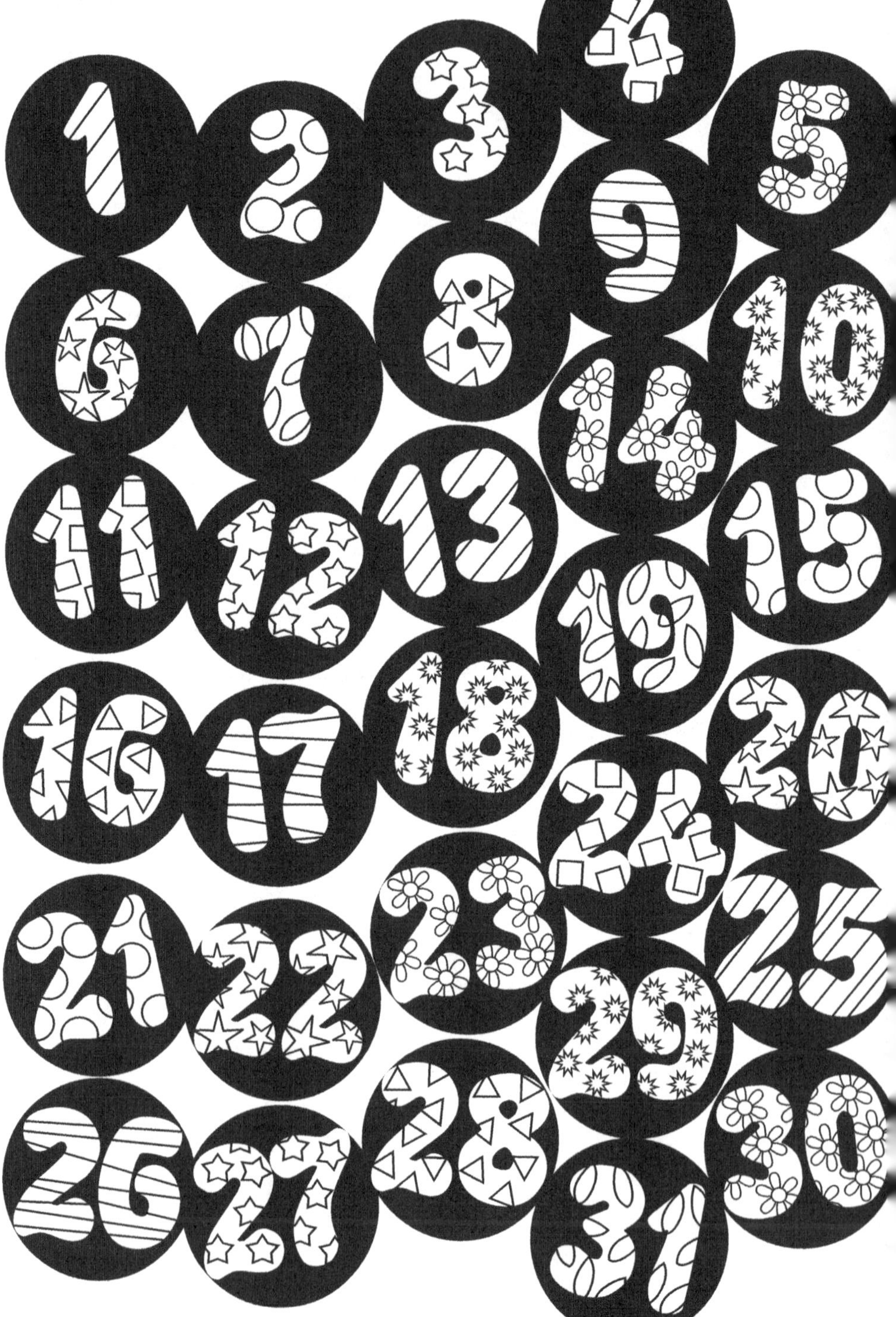

Month/year:

Goal/habit:

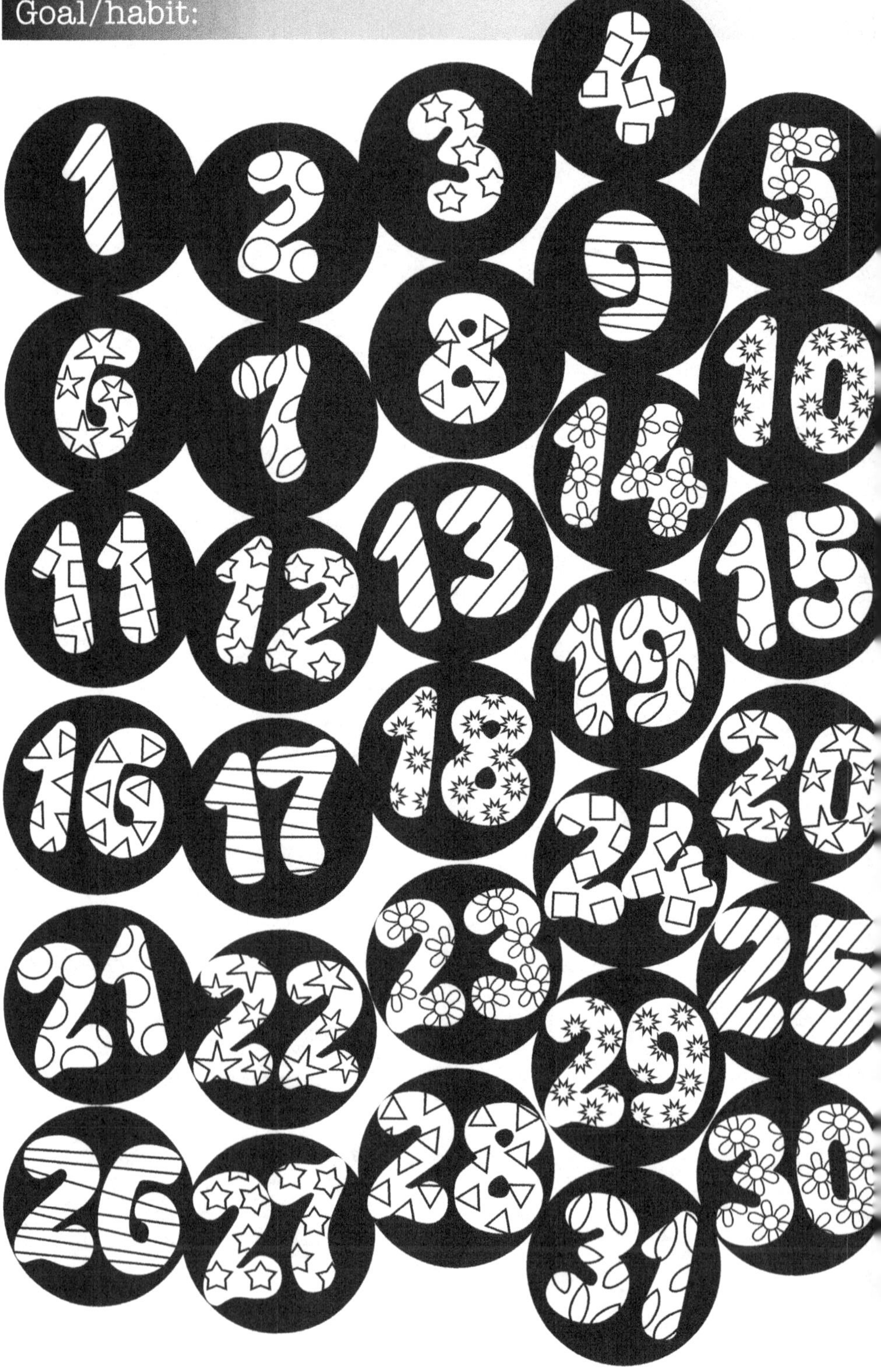

Month/year:

Goal/habit:

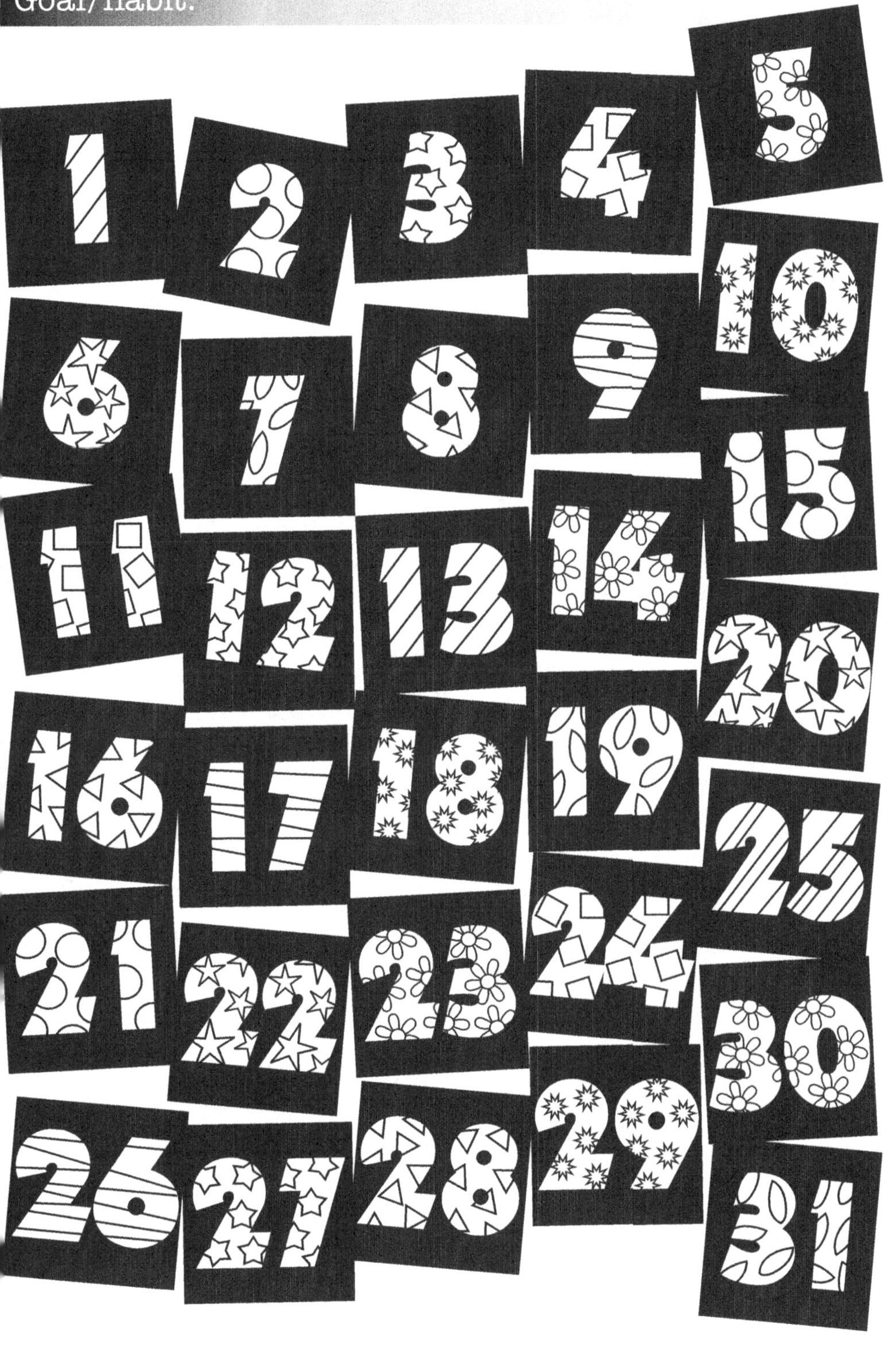

Month/year:

Goal/habit:

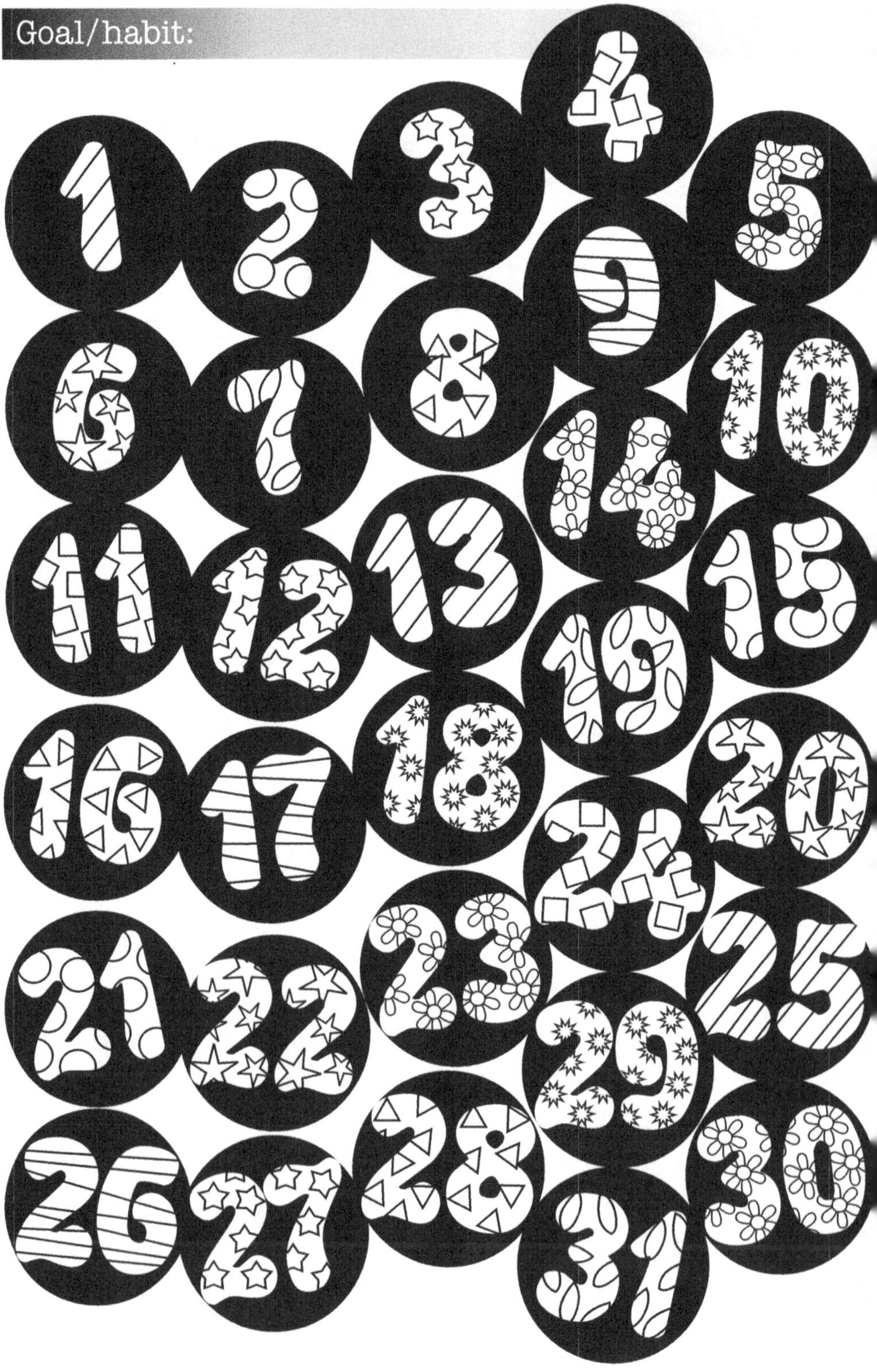

Month/year:

Goal/habit:

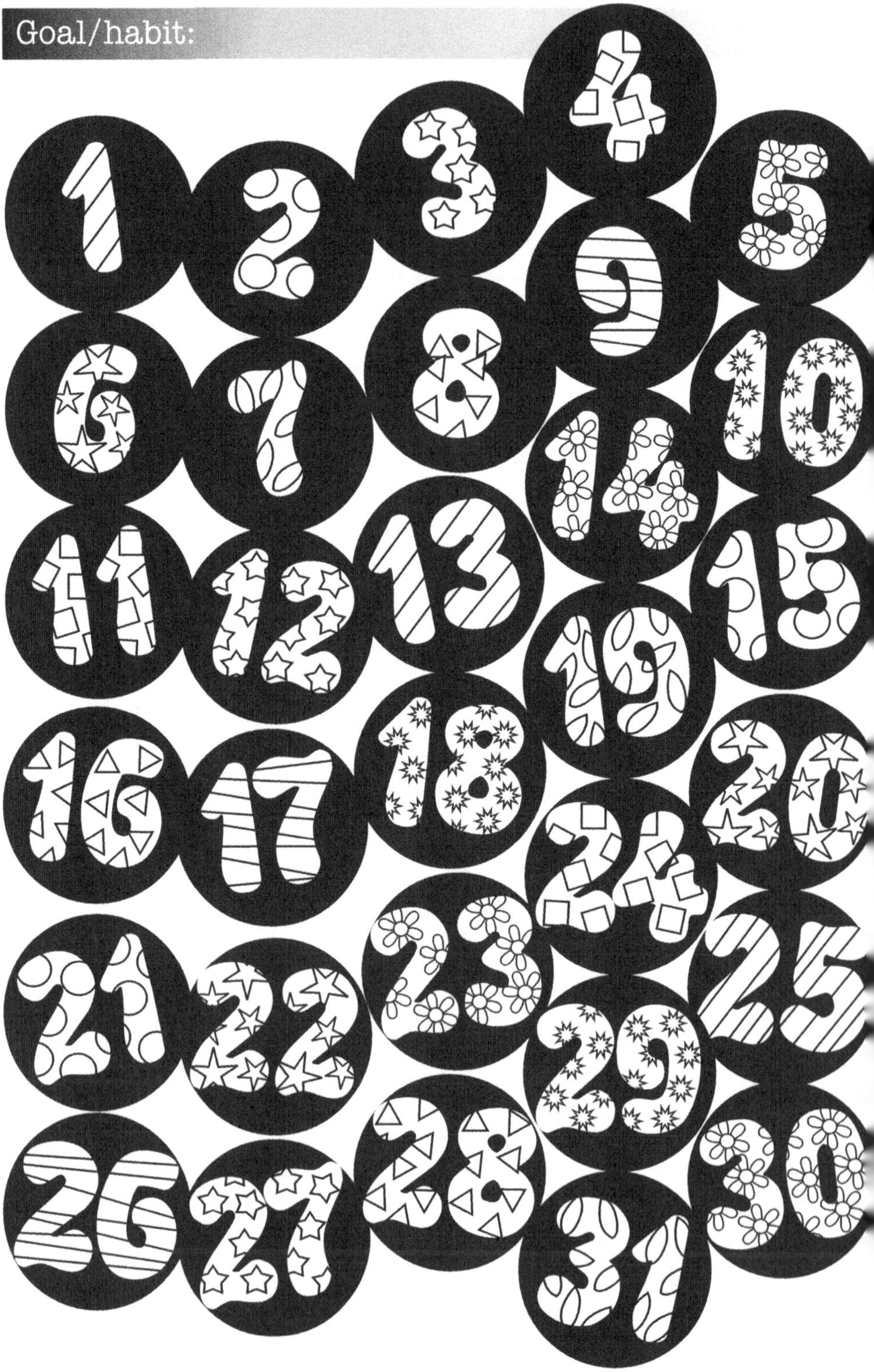

Month/year:

Goal/habit:

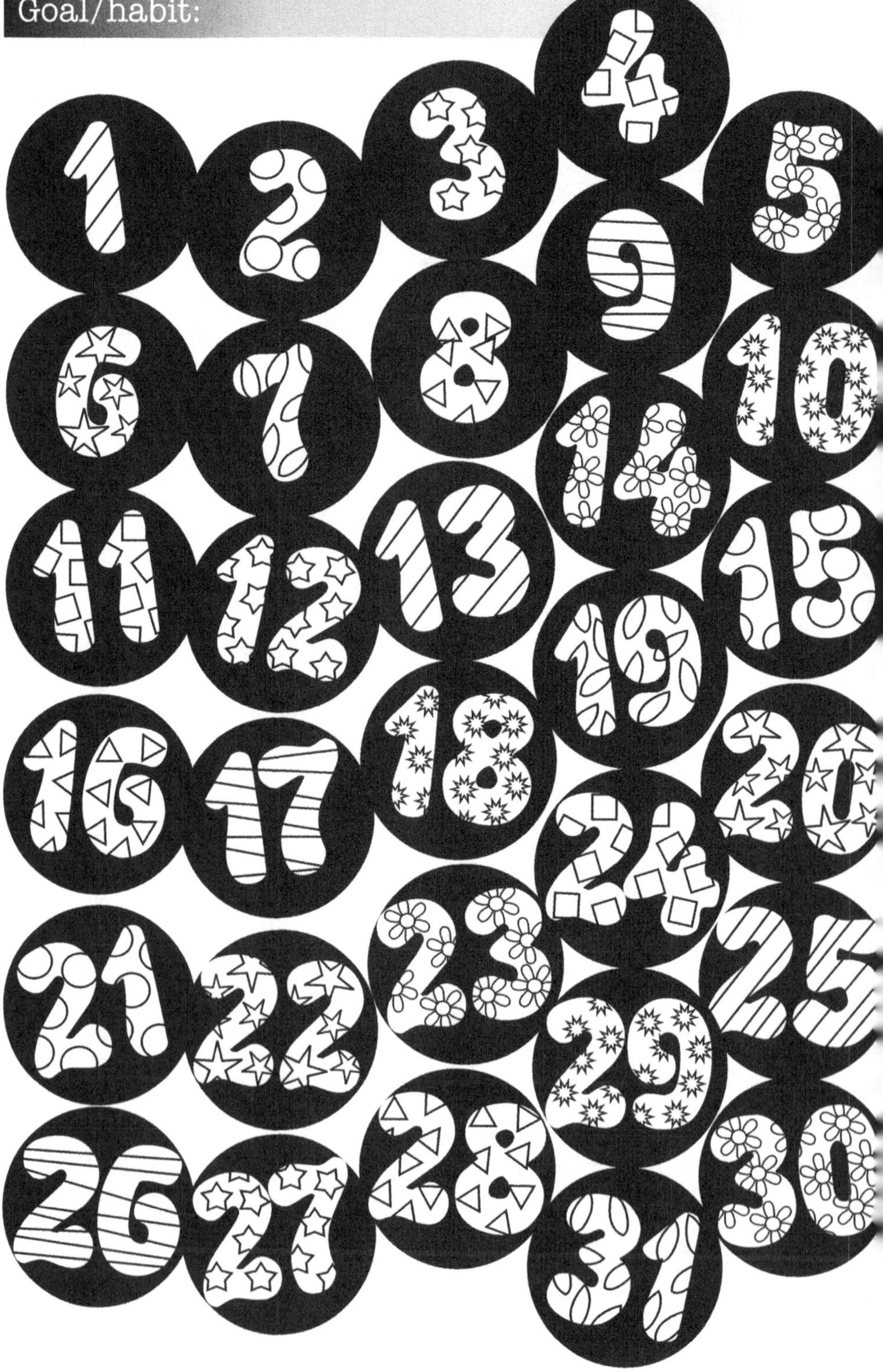

Month/year:

Goal/habit:

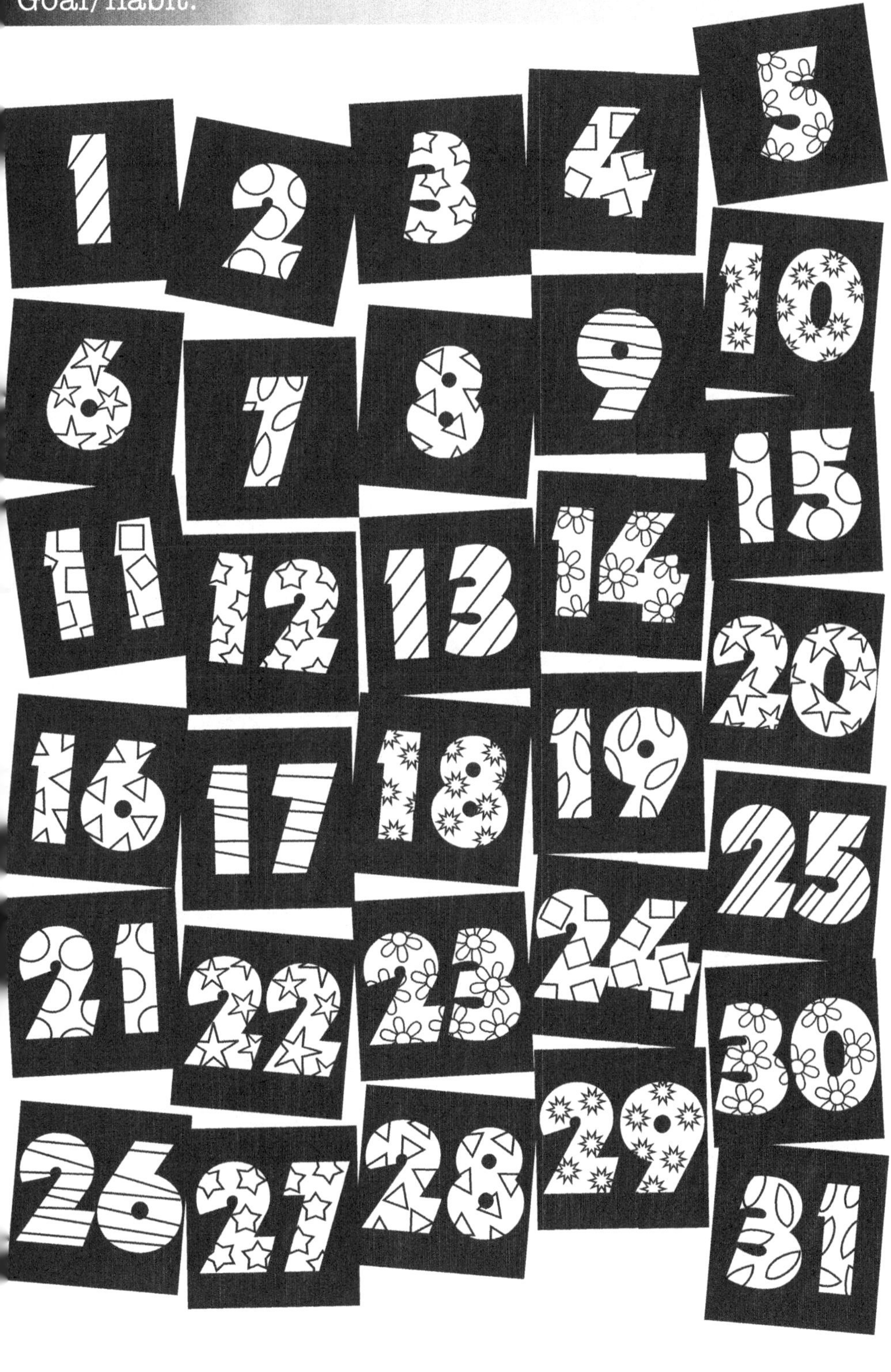

Month/year:

Goal/habit:

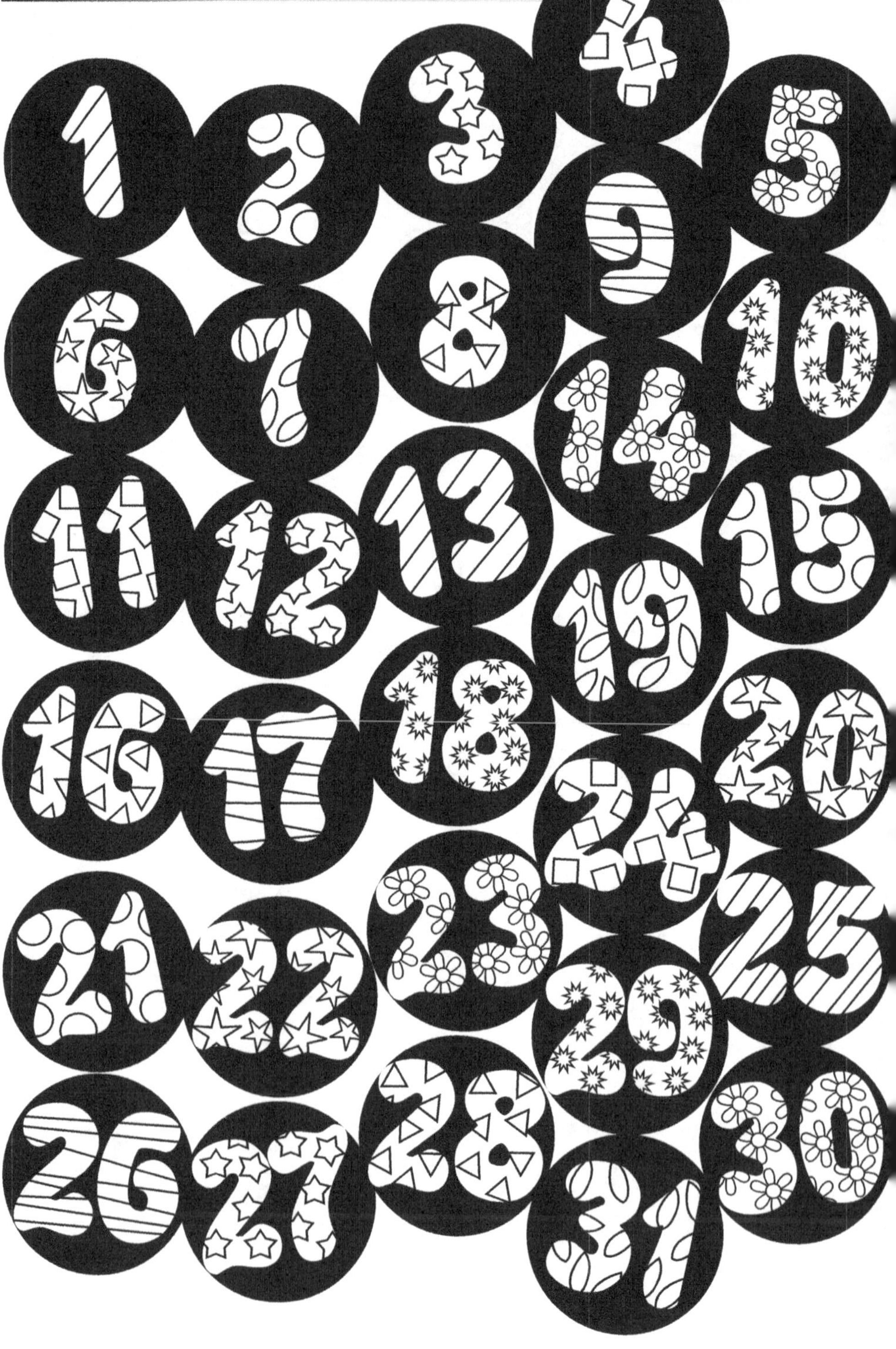

Month/year:

Goal/habit:

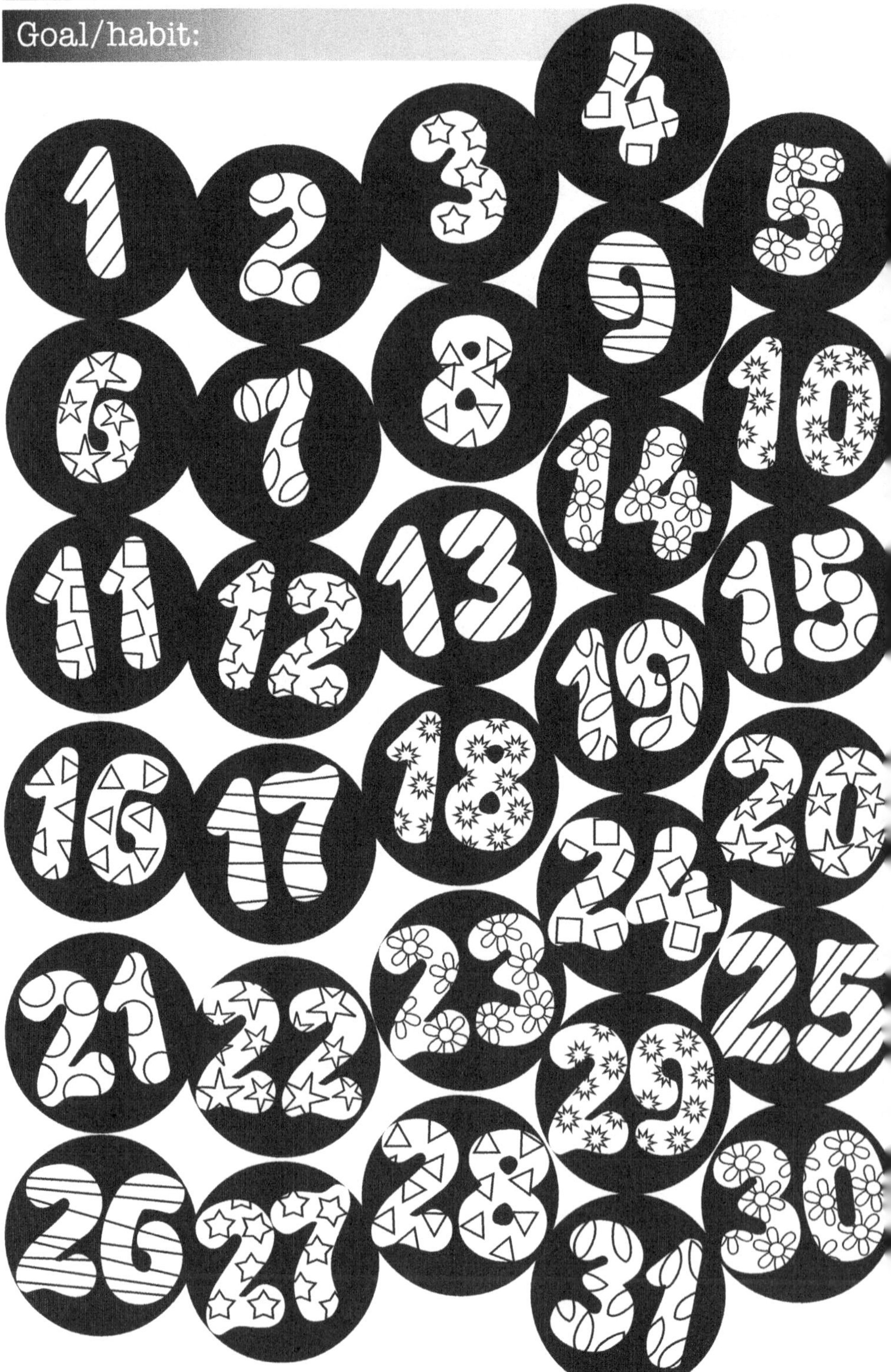

Month/year:

Goal/habit:

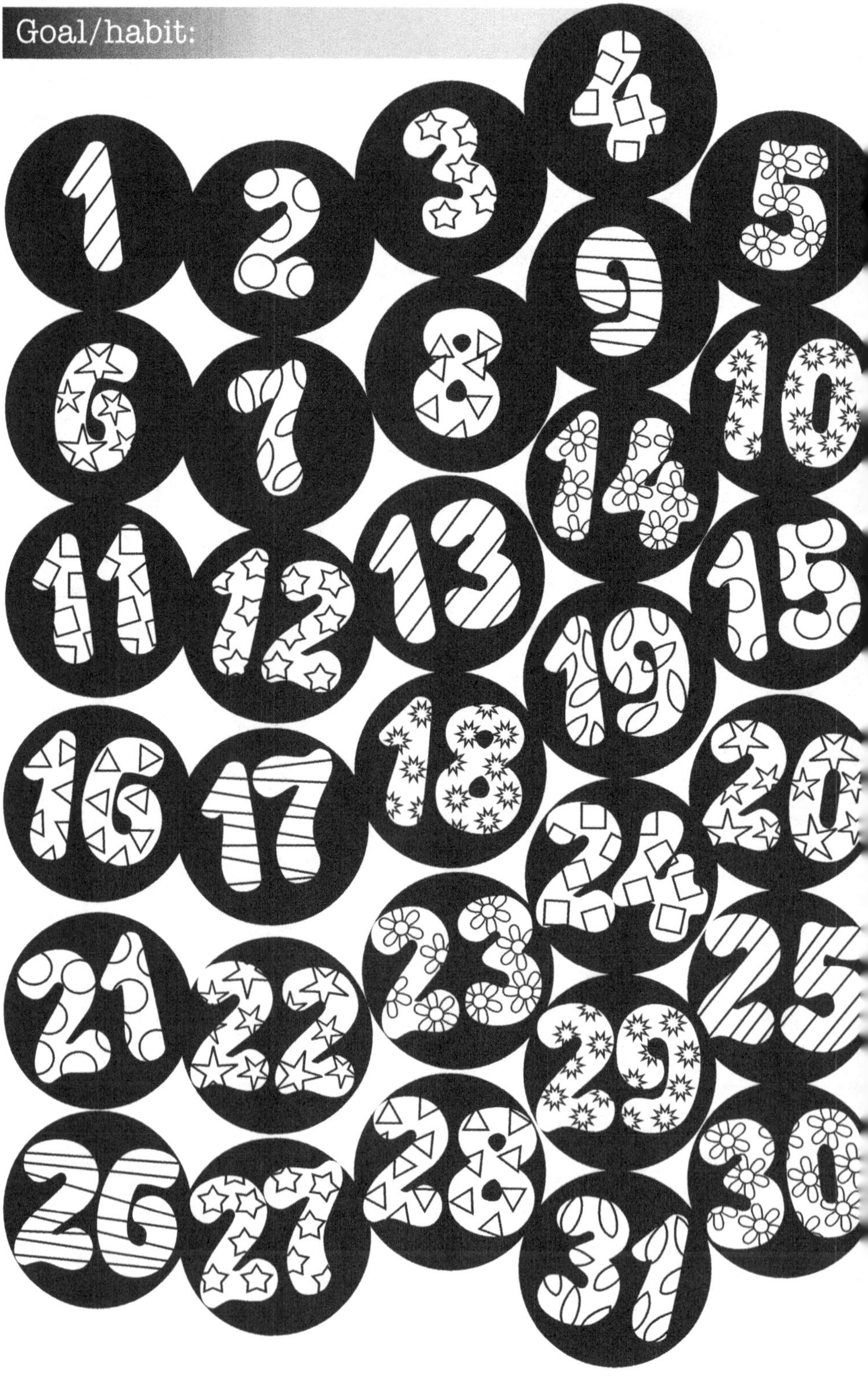

Month/year:

Goal/habit:

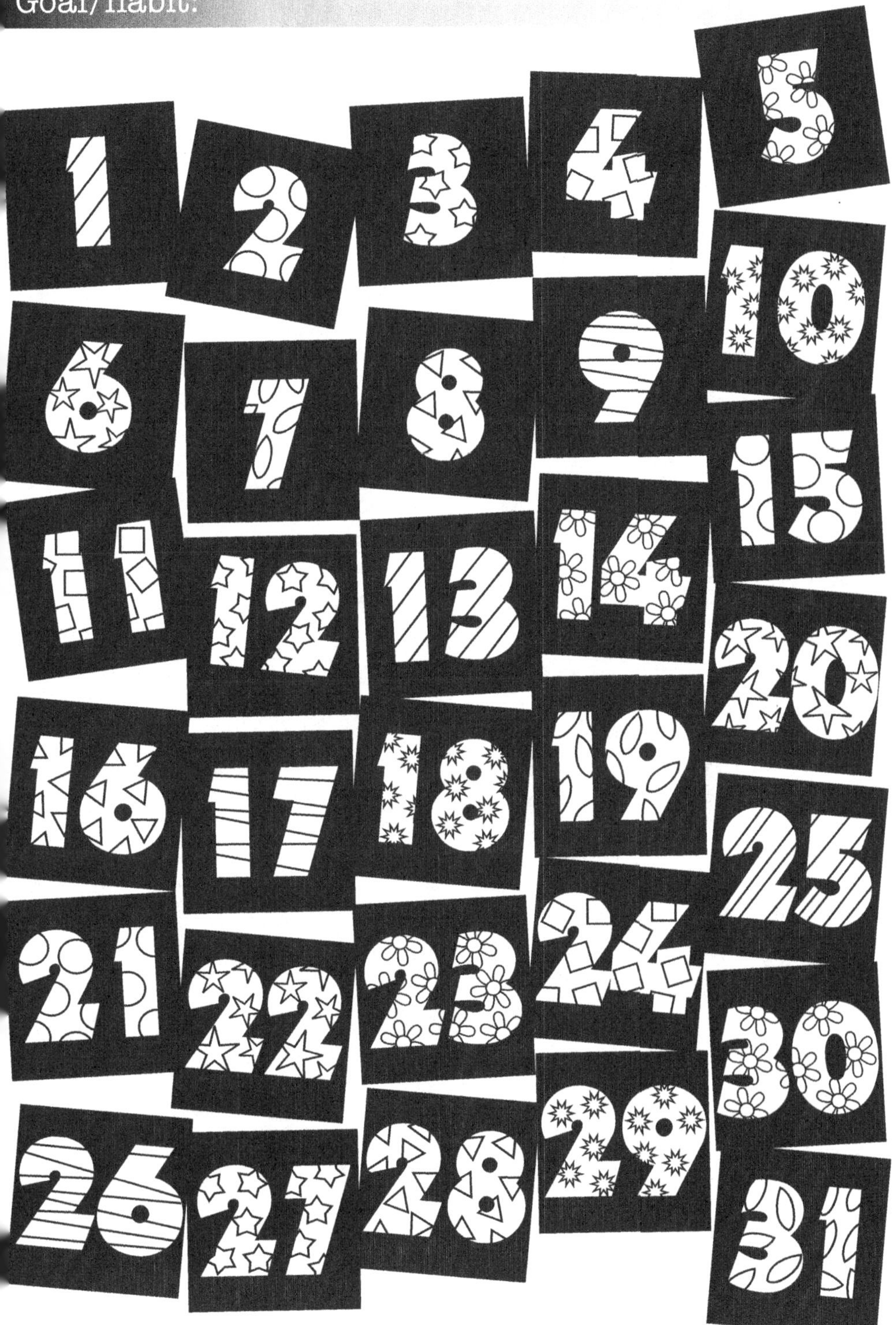

Month/year:

Goal/habit:

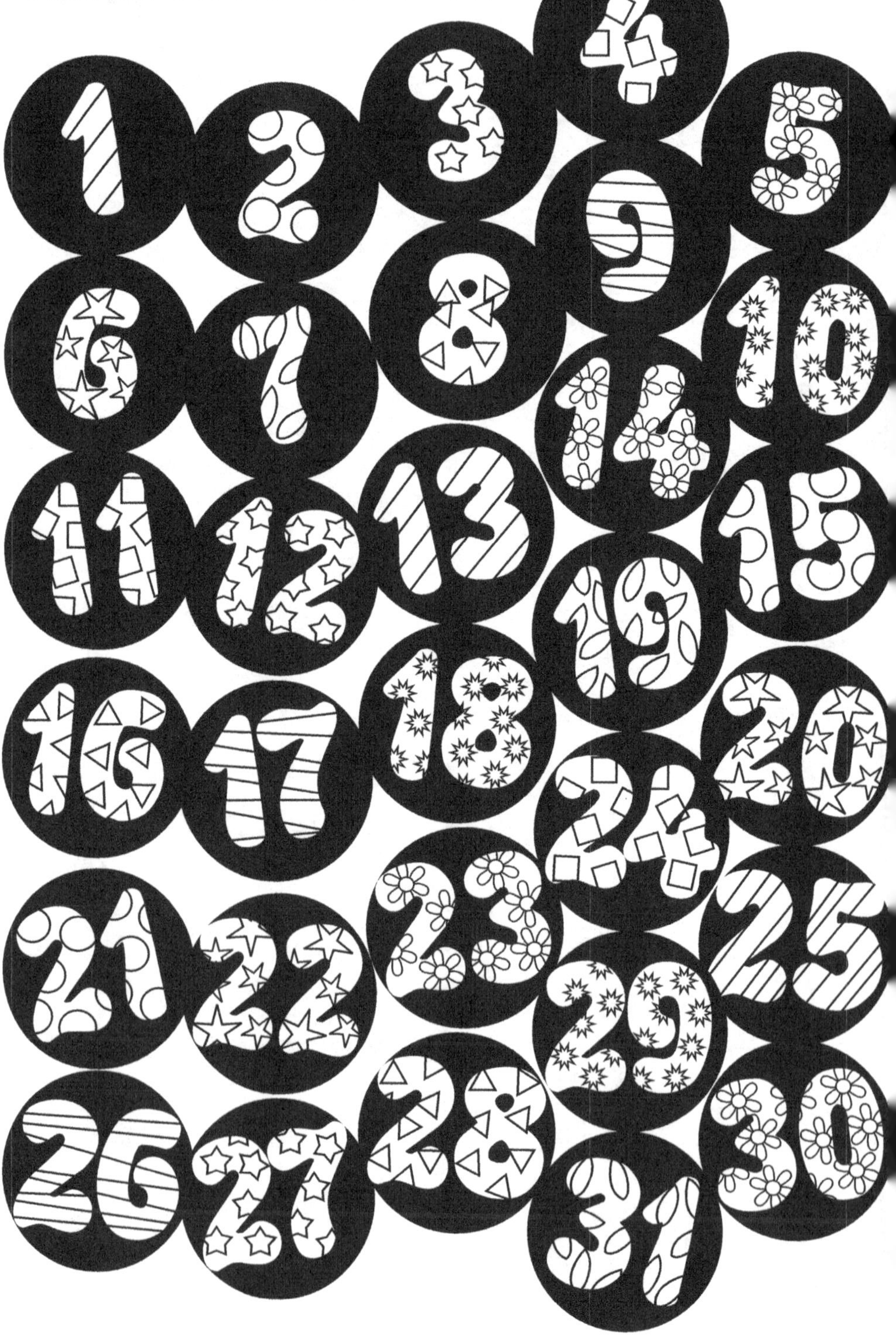

Month/year:

Goal/habit:

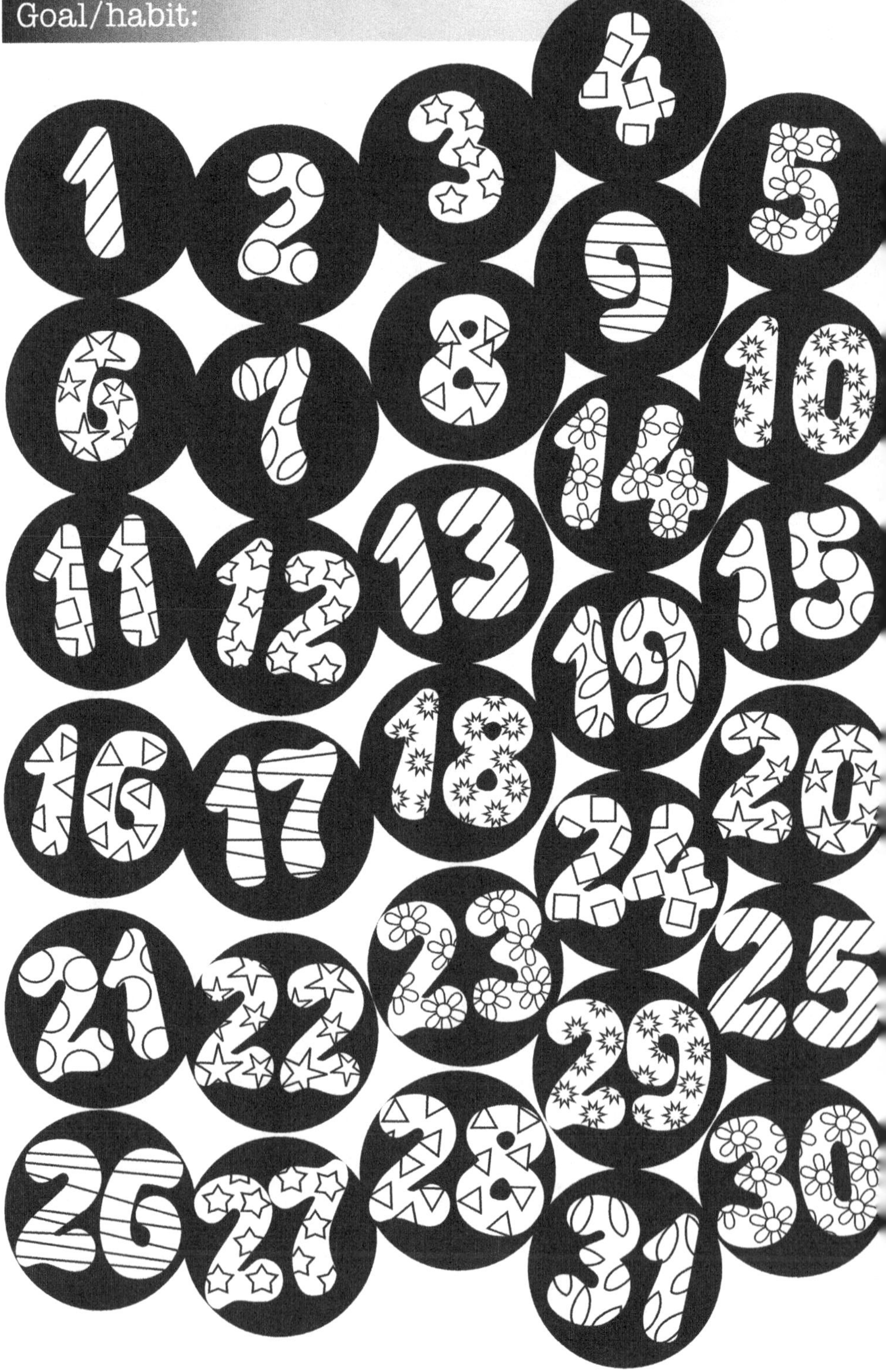

Month/year:

Goal/habit:

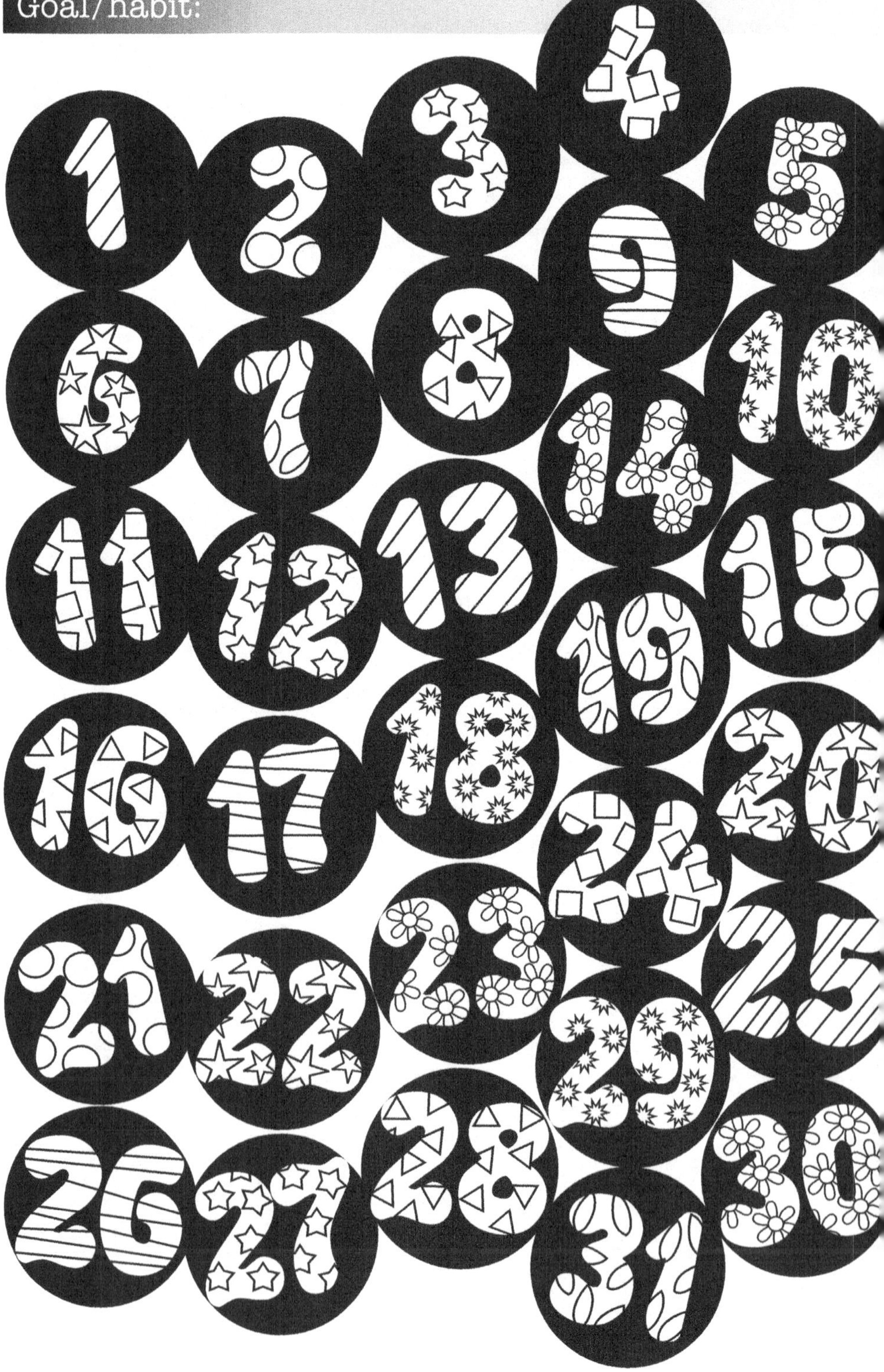

Month/year:

Goal/habit:

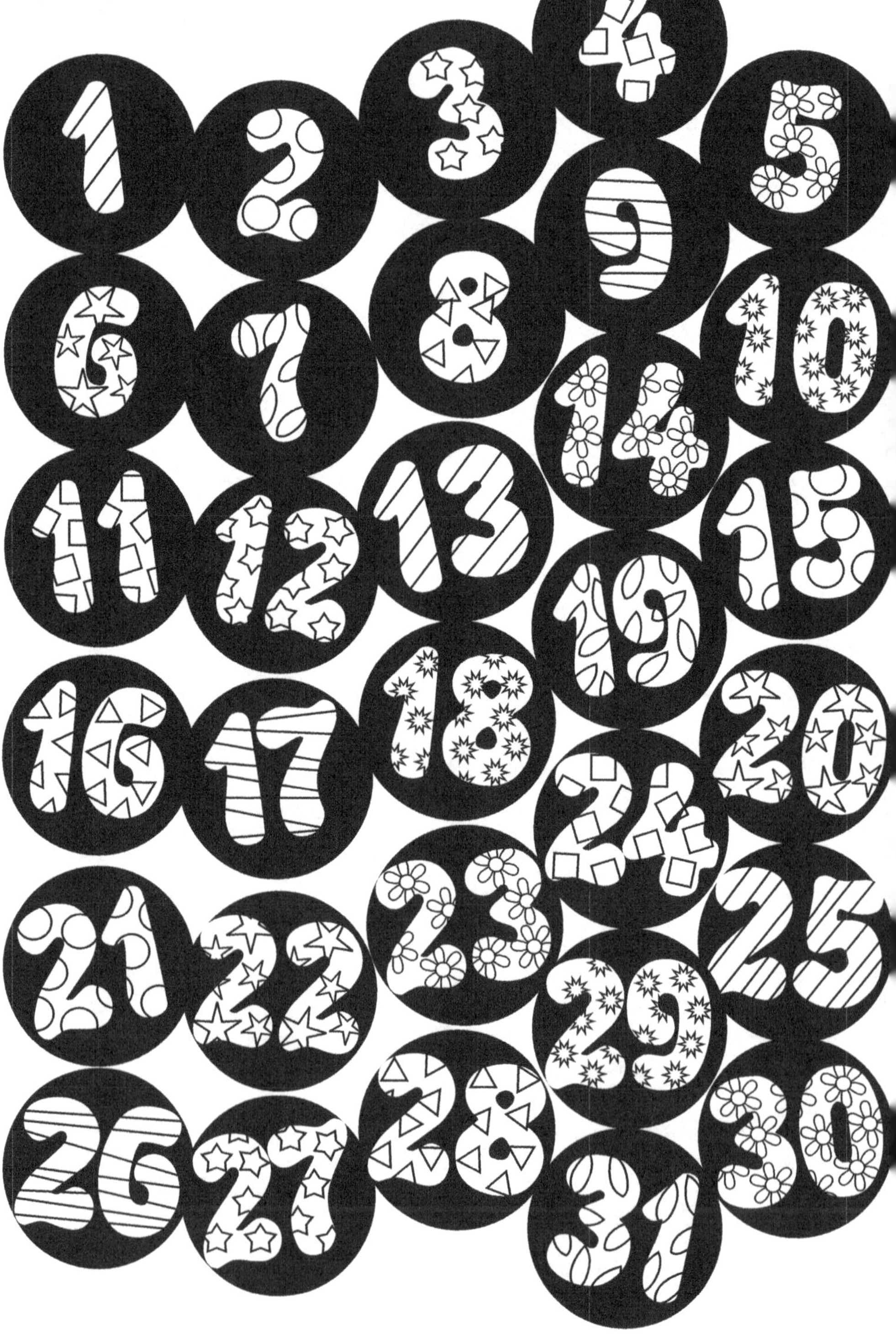

Month/year:

Goal/habit:

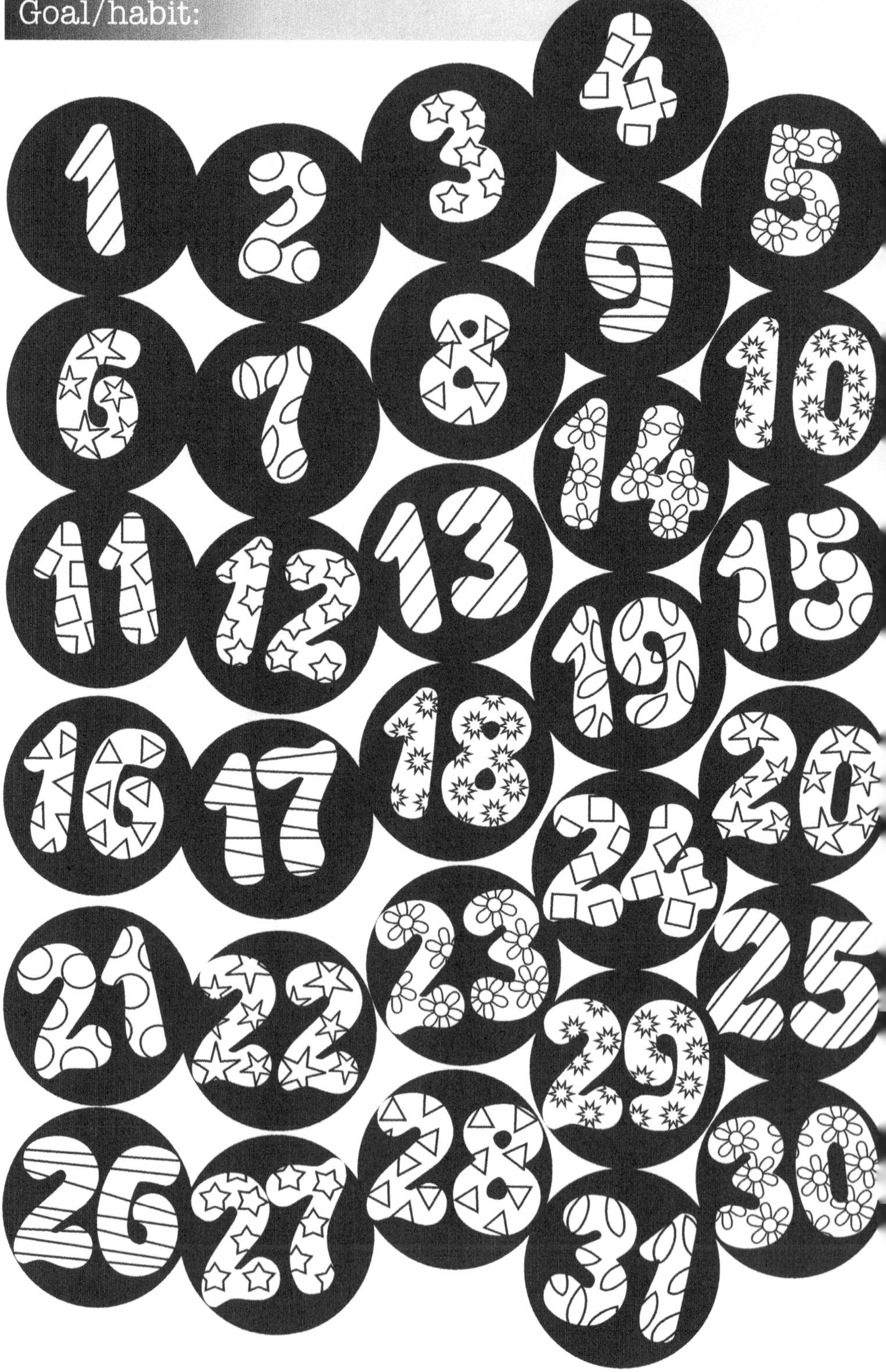

Month/year:

Goal/habit:

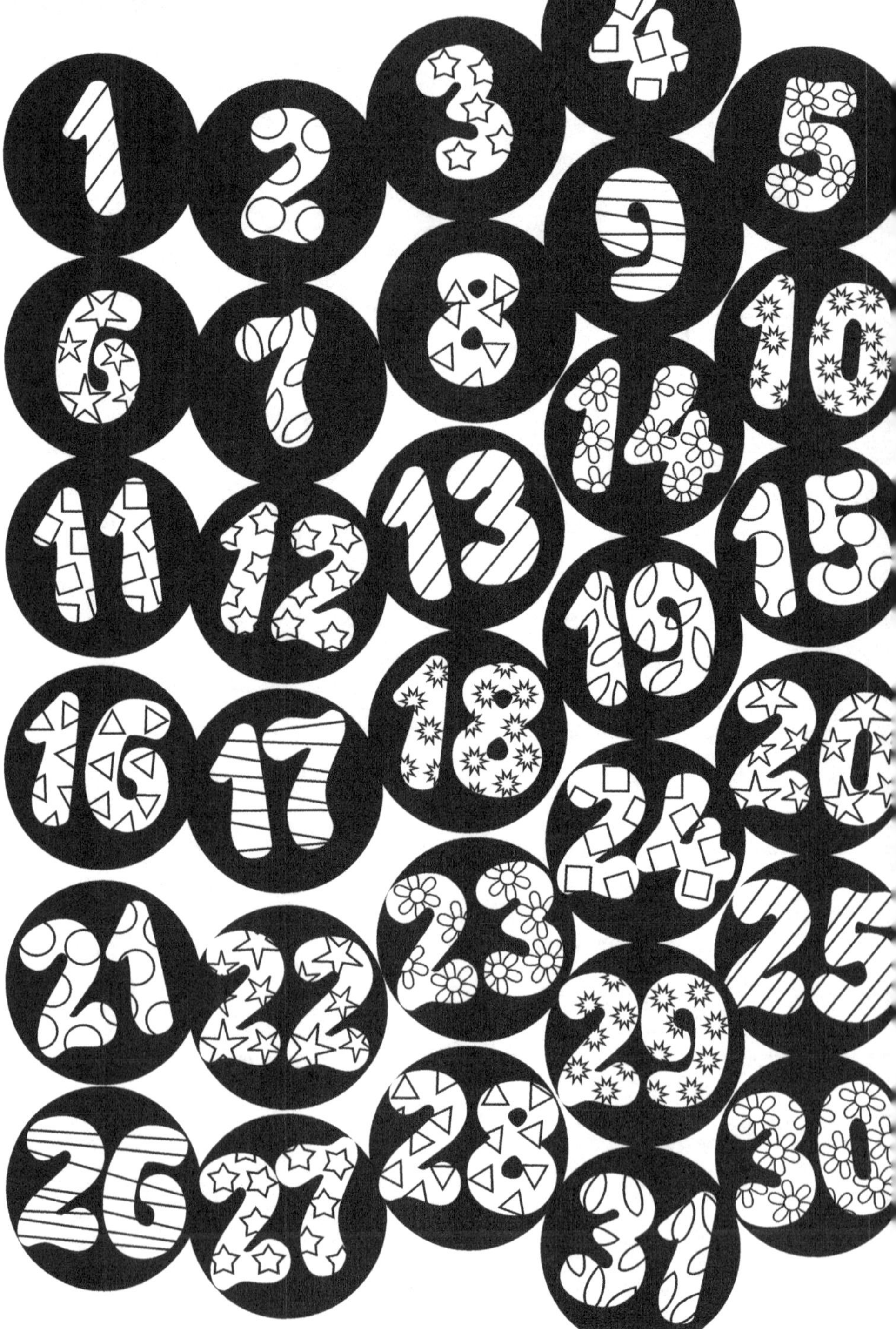

Month/year:

Goal/habit:

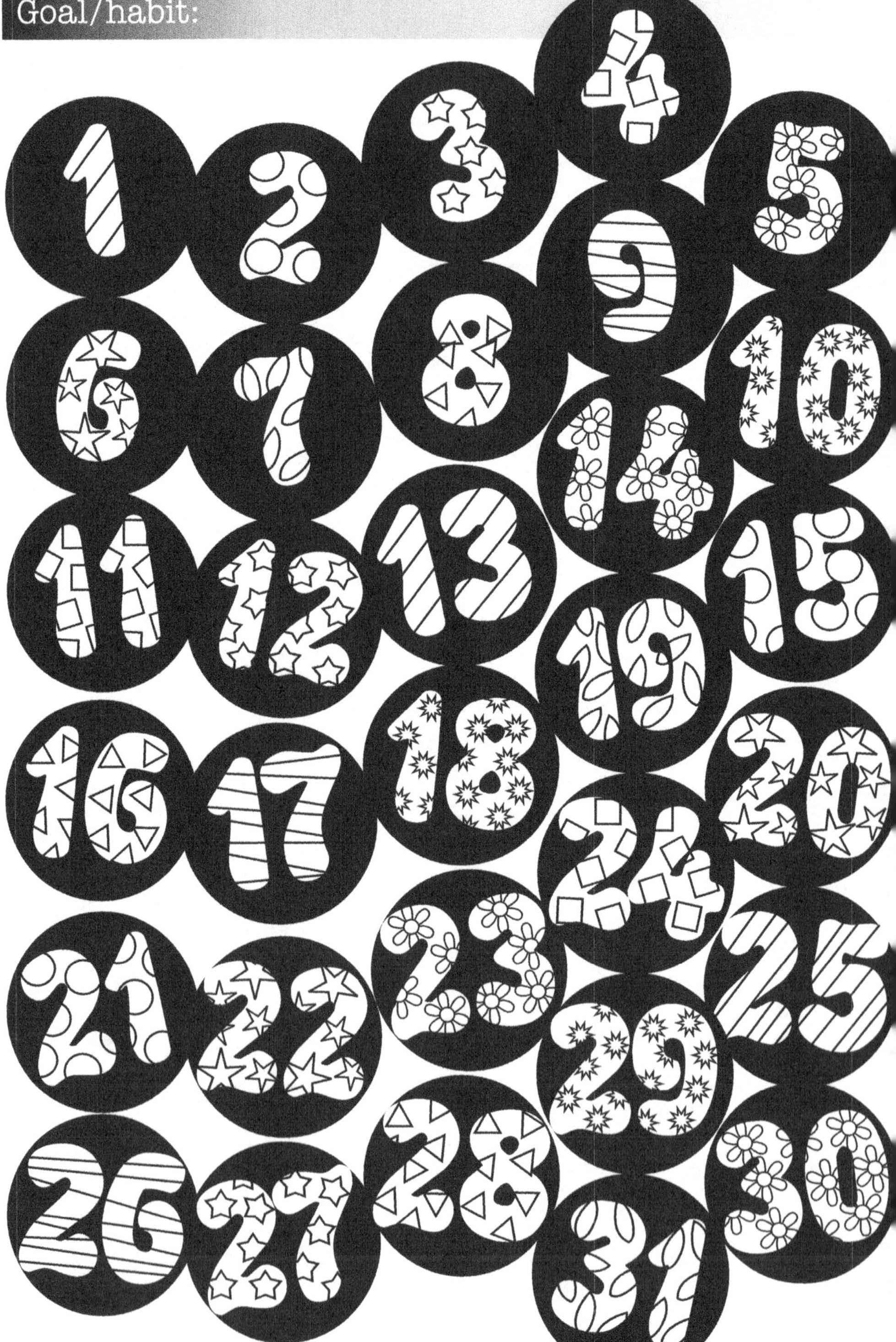

Month/year:

Goal/habit:

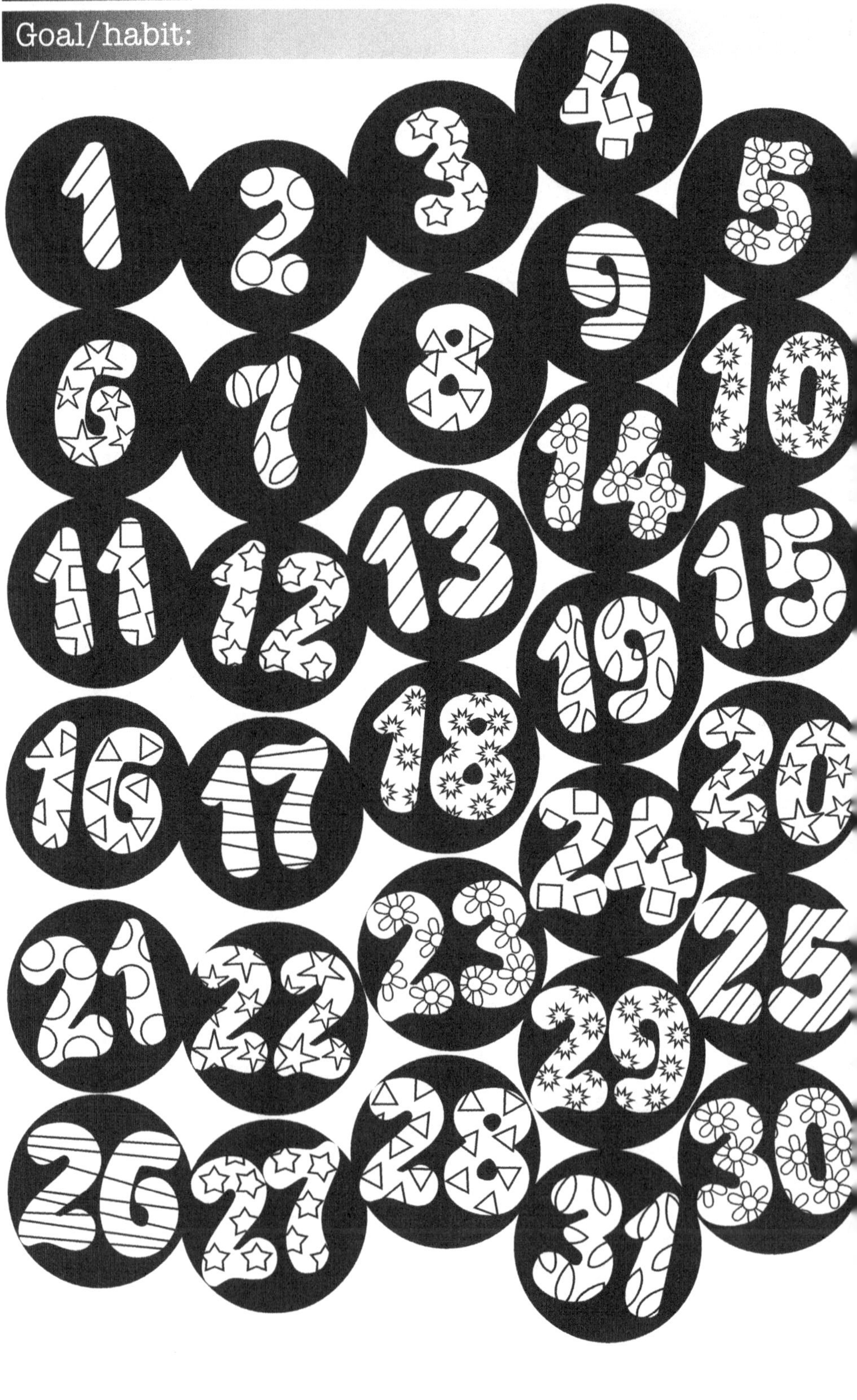

Month/year:

Goal/habit:

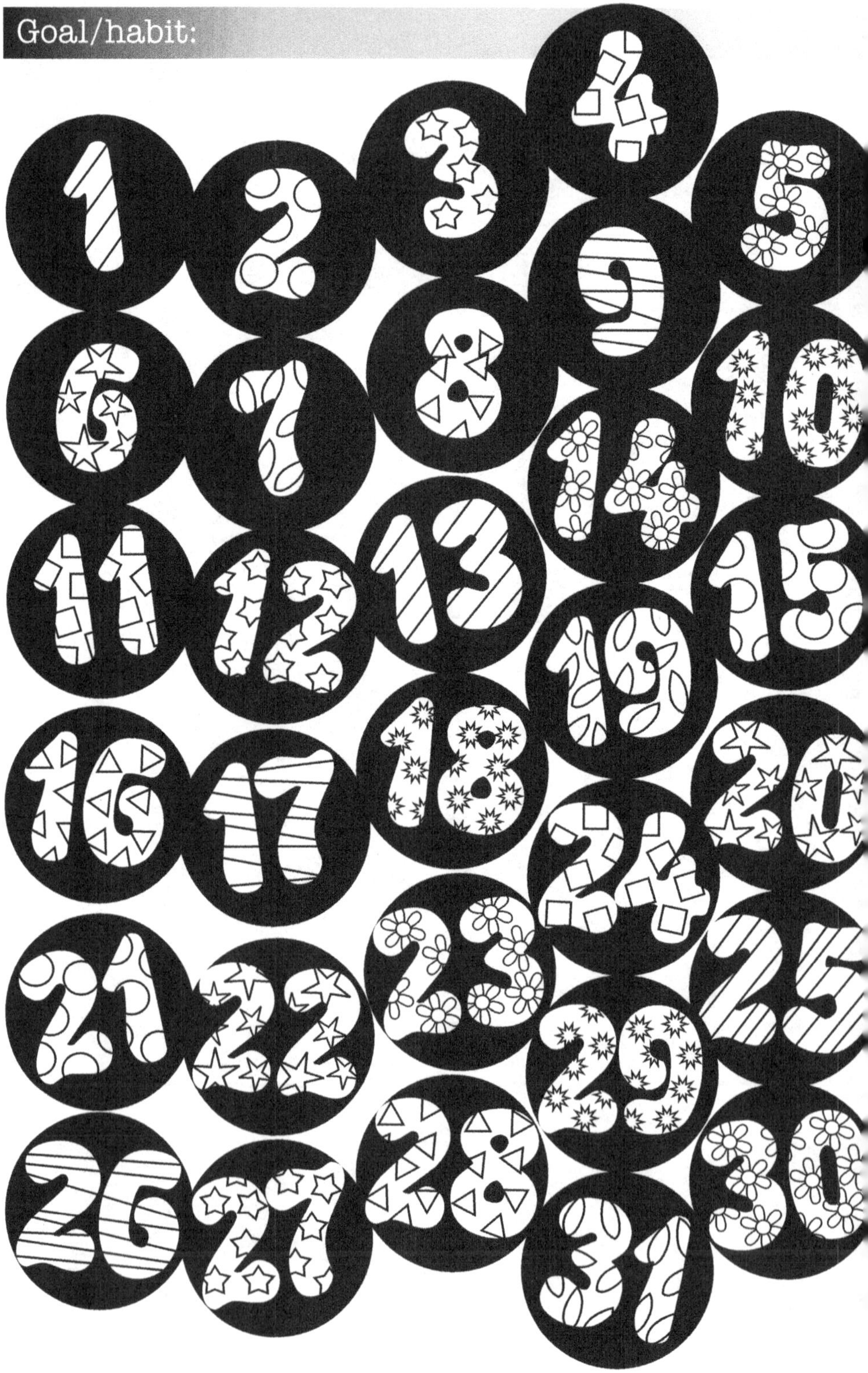

Month/year:

Goal/habit:

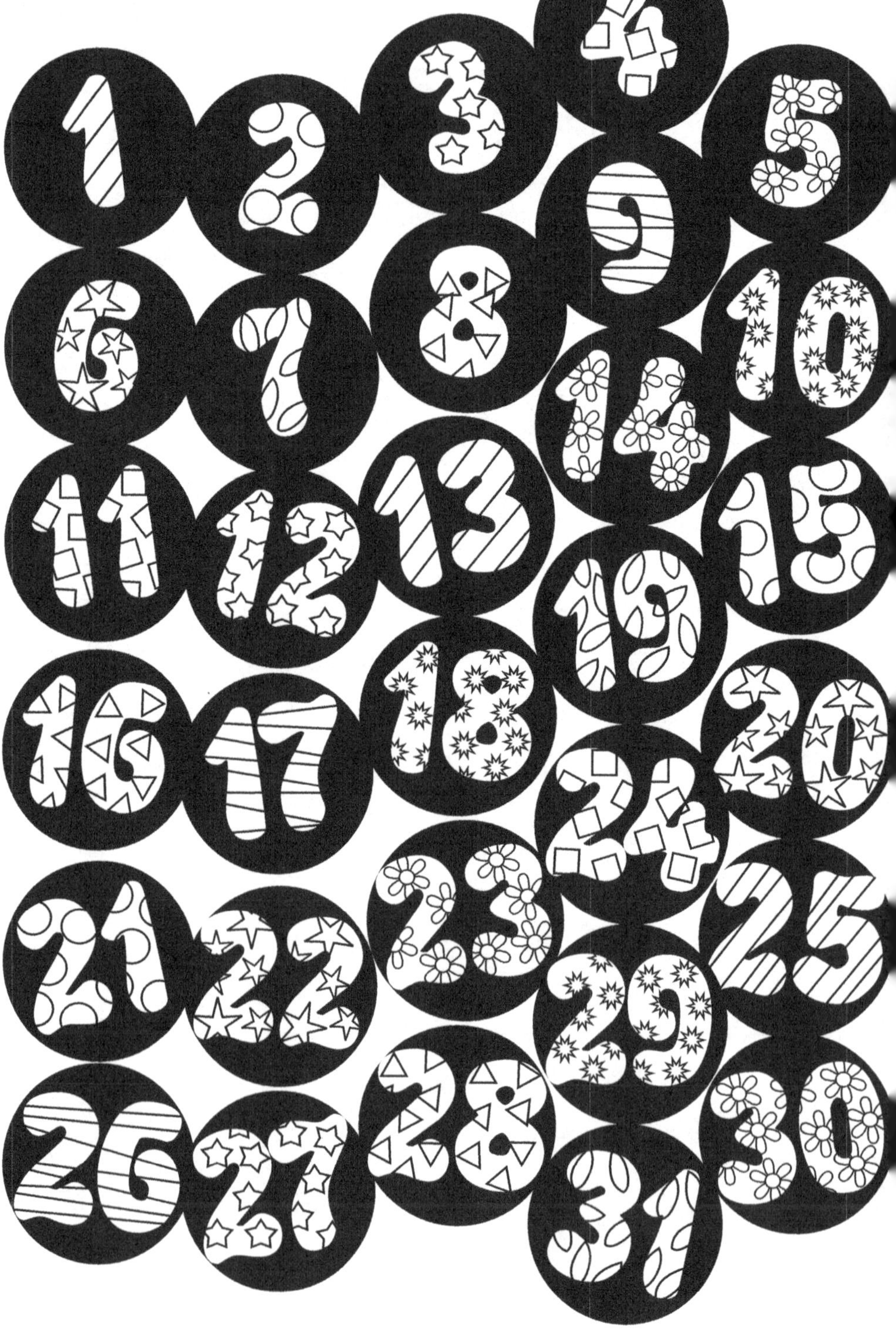

Month/year:

Goal/habit:

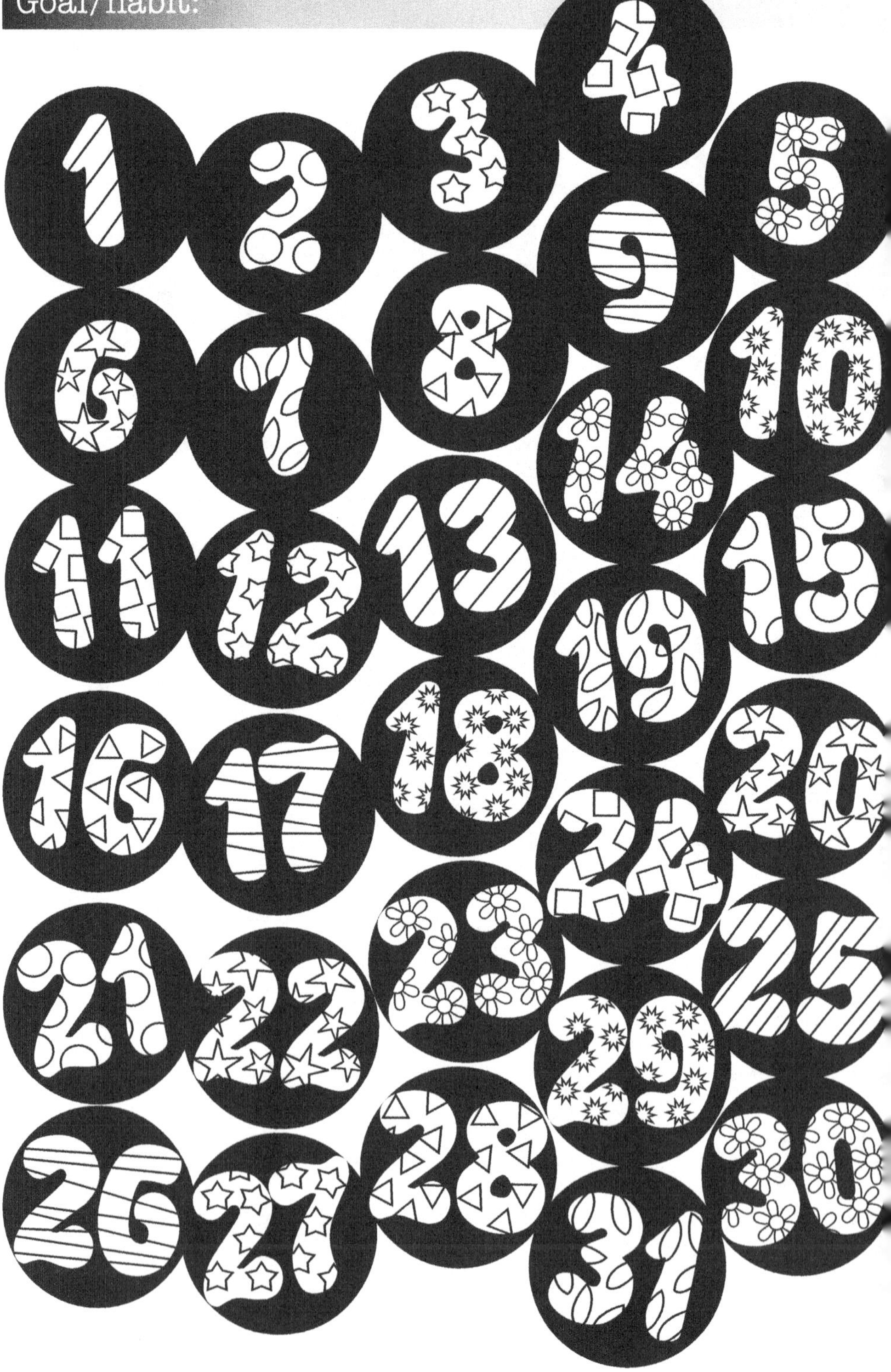

Month/year:

Goal/habit:

Month/year:

Goal/habit:

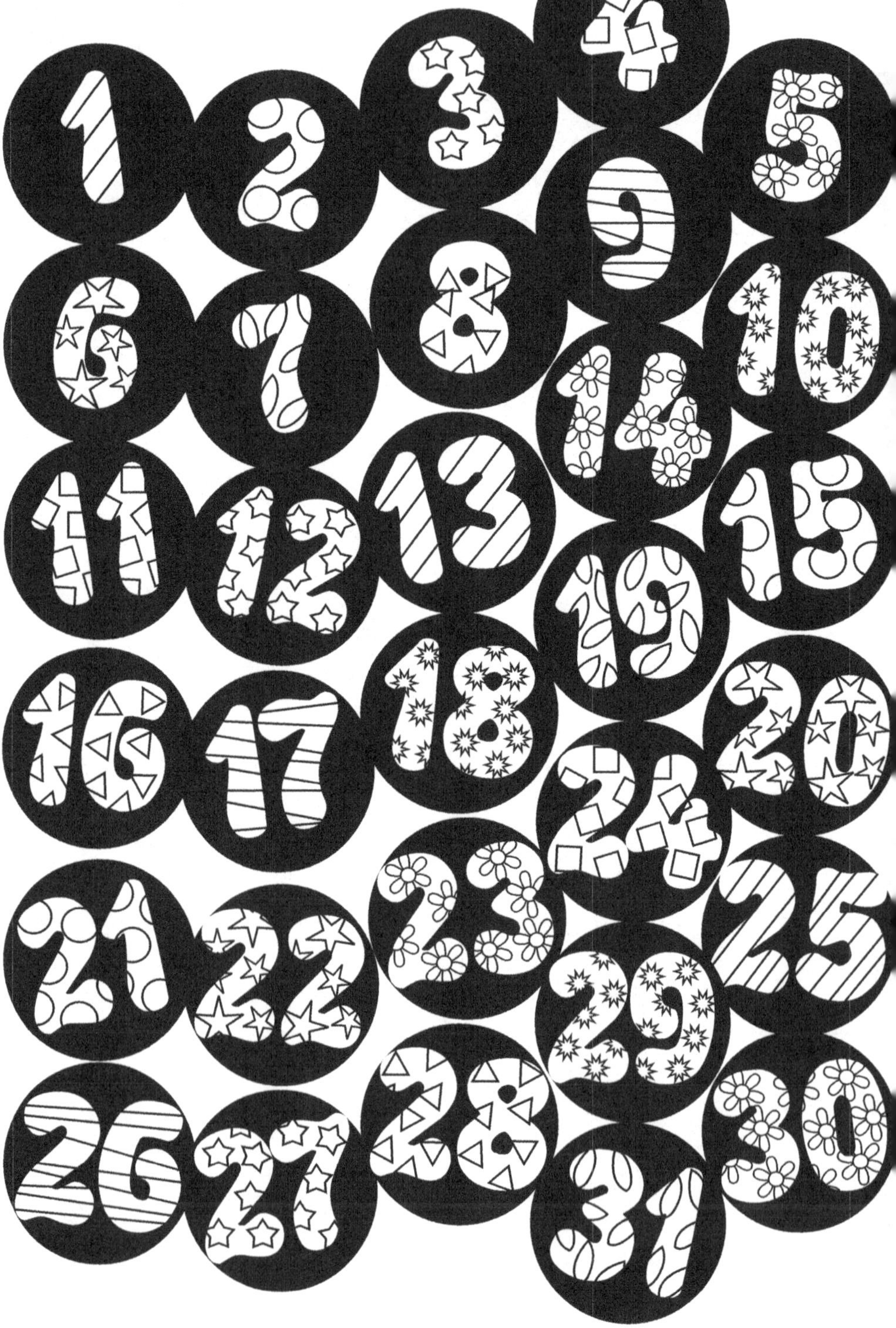

Month/year:

Goal/habit:

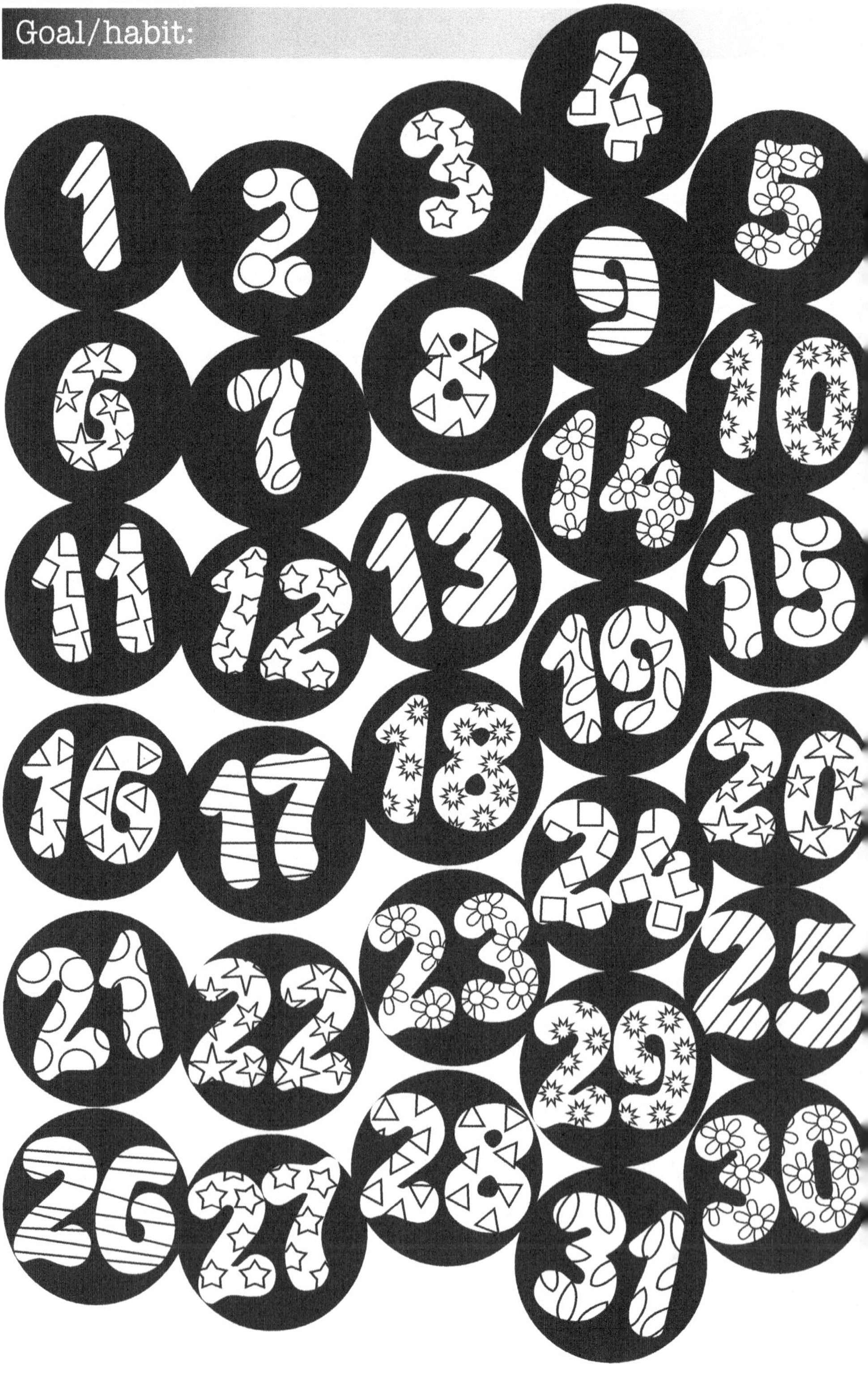

Month/year:

Goal/habit:

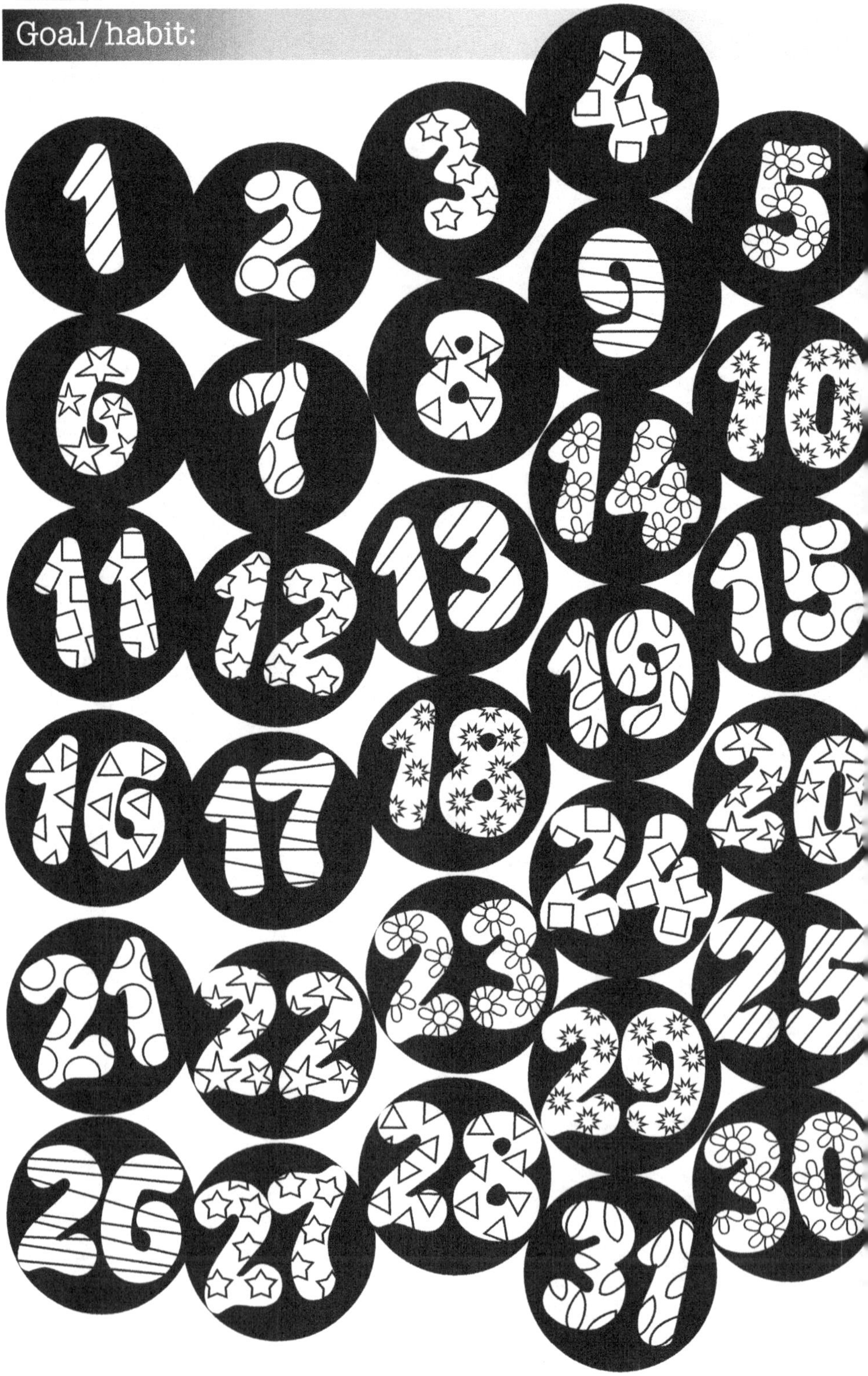

Month/year:

Goal/habit:

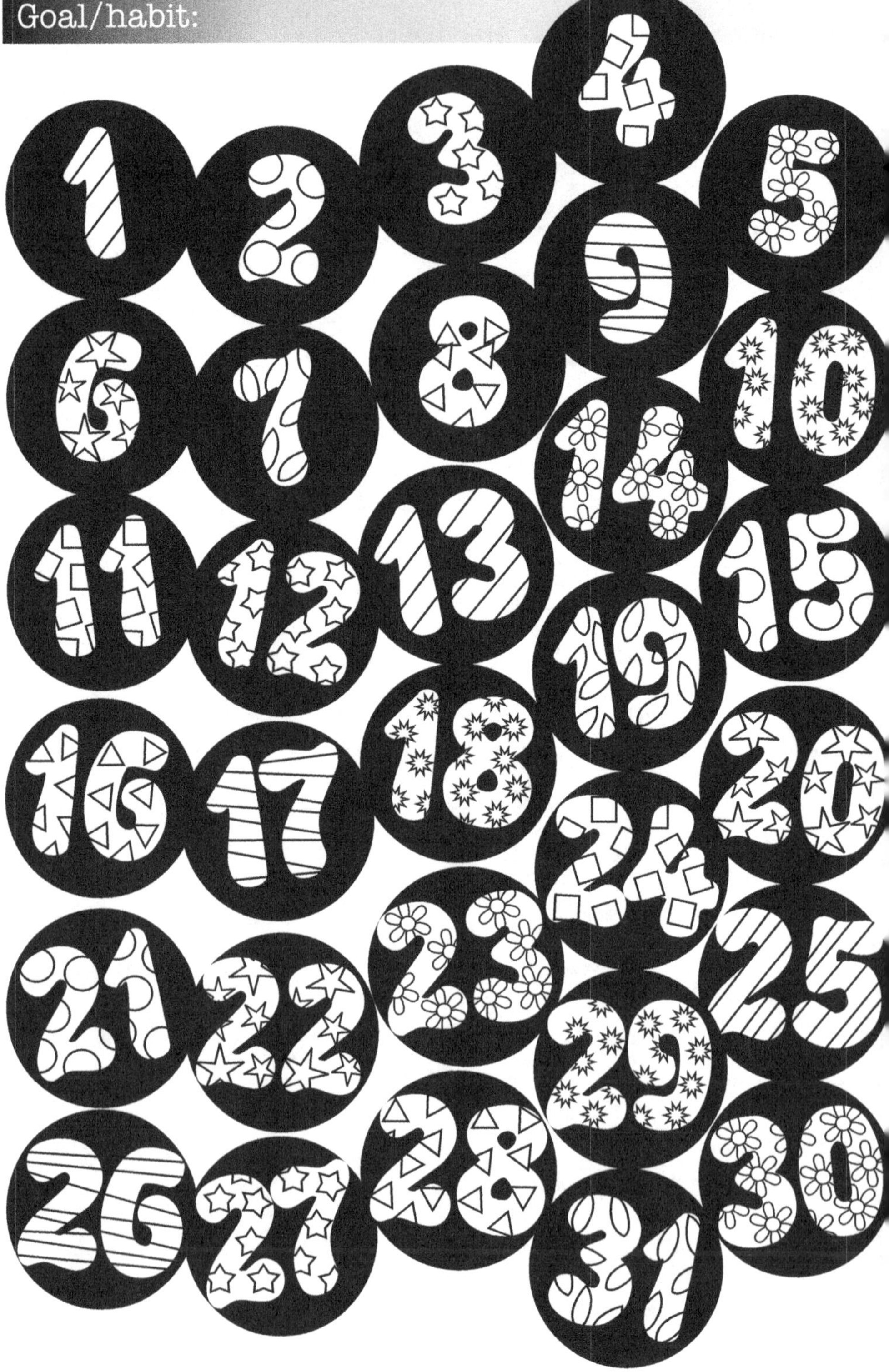

Month/year:

Goal/habit:

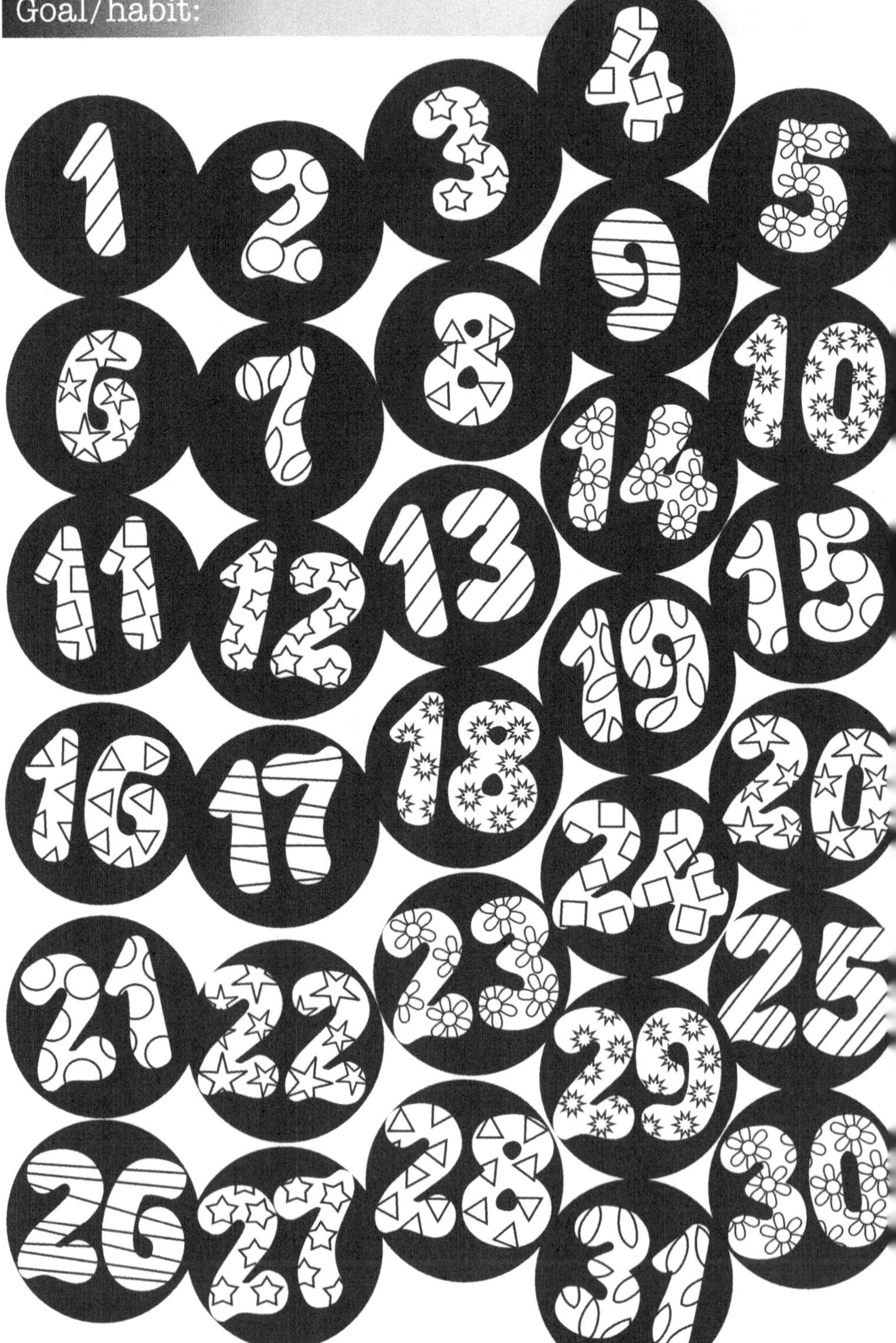

Made in the USA
Monee, IL
11 February 2023